ALEXANDER THE GREAT

ALEXANDER THE GREAT

Dennis Wepman

1986
CHELSEA HOUSE PUBLISHERS

NEW YORK
NEW HAVEN   PHILADELPHIA

SENIOR EDITOR: William P. Hansen
ASSOCIATE EDITORS: John Haney
Richard Mandell
Marian W. Taylor
EDITORIAL COORDINATOR: Karyn Gullen Browne
EDITORIAL STAFF: Pierre Hauser
Perry Scott King
John Selfridge
Bert Yaeger
ART DIRECTOR: Susan Lusk
LAYOUT: Irene Friedman
ART ASSISTANTS: Carol McDougall
Tenaz Mehta
COVER DESIGN: Peter McCaffrey
PICTURE RESEARCH: Ian Ensign

First Printing

Library of Congress Cataloging in Publication Data

Wepman, Dennis. ALEXANDER THE GREAT

(World Leaders Past & Present)
Bibliography: p.
Includes index
   1. Alexander, the Great, 356–323 B.C.—Juvenile literature. 2.
Greece—History—Macedonian Expansion, 359–322 B.C.—Juvenile
literature. 3. Generals—Greece—Biography—Juvenile literature. 4.
Greece—Kings and rulers—Biography—Juvenile literature. [1. Alexander,
the Great, 356–323 B.C. 2. Kings, queens, rulers, etc. I. Title. II. Series.
DF234.W47   1986   938'.07'0924 [B] [92]   85-16674

ISBN 0-87754-594-4

Chelsea House Publishers

Harold Steinberg, Chairman & Publisher
Susan Lusk, Vice President
A Division of Chelsea House Educational Communications, Inc.

Chelsea House Publishers
133 Christopher Street
New York, N.Y. 10014

Contents

CHELSEA HOUSE PUBLISHERS

WORLD LEADERS PAST & PRESENT

ADENAUER
ALEXANDER THE GREAT
MARK ANTONY
KING ARTHUR
KEMAL ATATÜRK
CLEMENT ATTLEE
BEGIN
BEN GURION
BISMARCK
LEON BLUM
BOLÍVAR
CESARE BORGIA
BRANDT
BREZHNEV
CAESAR
CALVIN
CASTRO
CATHERINE THE GREAT
CHARLEMAGNE
CHIANG KAI-SHEK
CHOU EN-LAI
CHURCHILL
CLEMENCEAU
CLEOPATRA
CORTEZ
CROMWELL
DANTON
DE GAULLE
DE VALERA
DISRAELI
EISENHOWER
ELEANOR OF AQUITAINE
QUEEN ELIZABETH I
FERDINAND AND ISABELLA

FRANCO
FREDERICK THE GREAT
INDIRA GANDHI
GANDHI
GARIBALDI
GENGHIS KHAN
GLADSTONE
HAMMARSKJÖLD
HENRY VIII
HENRY OF NAVARRE
HINDENBURG
HITLER
HO CHI MINH
KING HUSSEIN
IVAN THE TERRIBLE
ANDREW JACKSON
JEFFERSON
JOAN OF ARC
POPE JOHN XXIII
LYNDON JOHNSON
BENITO JUÁREZ
JFK
KENYATTA
KHOMEINI
KHRUSHCHEV
MARTIN LUTHER KING
KISSINGER
LENIN
LINCOLN
LLOYD GEORGE
LOUIS XIV
LUTHER
JUDAS MACCABEUS

MAO
MARY, QUEEN OF SCOTS
GOLDA MEIR
METTERNICH
MUSSOLINI
NAPOLEON
NASSER
NEHRU
NERO
NICHOLAS II
NIXON
NKRUMAH
PERICLES
PERÓN
QADDAFI
ROBESPIERRE
ELEANOR ROOSEVELT
FDR
THEODORE ROOSEVELT
SADAT
SUN YAT-SEN
STALIN
TAMERLAINE
THATCHER
TITO
TROTSKY
TRUDEAU
TRUMAN
QUEEN VICTORIA
WASHINGTON
CHAIM WEIZMANN
WOODROW WILSON
XERXES

Further titles in preparation

ON LEADERSHIP

Arthur M. Schlesinger, jr.

LEADERSHIP, it may be said, is really what makes the world go round. Love no doubt smooths the passage; but love is a private transaction between consenting adults. Leadership is a public trans- action with history. The idea of leadership affirms the capacity of individuals to move, inspire and mobilize masses of people so that they act together in pursuit of an end. Sometimes leadership serves good purposes, sometimes bad; but whether the end is benign or evil, great leaders are those men and women who leave their per- sonal stamp on history.

Now, the very concept of leadership implies the proposition that individuals can make a difference. This proposition has never been universally accepted. From classical times to the present day, eminent thinkers have regarded individuals as no more than the agents and pawns of larger forces, whether the gods and goddesses of the ancient world or, in the modern era, race, class, nation, the dialectic, the will of the people, the spirit of the times, history itself. Against such forces, the individual dwindles into insignificance.

So contends the thesis of historical determinism. Tolstoy's great novel *War and Peace* offers a famous statement of the case. Why, Tolstoy asked, did millions of men in the Napoleonic wars, denying their human feelings and their common sense, move back and forth across Europe slaughtering their fellows? "The war," Tolstoy answered, "was bound to happen simply because it was bound to happen." All prior history predetermined it. As for leaders, they, Tolstoy said, "are but the labels that serve to give a name to an end and, like labels, they have the least possible connection with the event." The greater the leader, "the more conspicuous the inevi- tability and the predestination of every act he commits." The leader, said Tolstoy, is "the slave of history."

Determinism takes many forms. Marxism is the determin- ism of class, Nazism the determinism of race. But the idea of men and women as the slaves of history runs athwart the deepest hu- man instincts. Rigid determinism abolishes the idea of human freedom—the assumption of free choice that underlies every move we make, every word we speak, every thought we think. It abolishes the idea of human responsibility, since it is manifestly unfair to reward or punish people for actions that are by definition beyond their control. No one can live consistently by any deterministic creed. The Marxist states prove this themselves by their extreme susceptibility to the cult of leadership.

More than that, history refutes the idea that individuals make no difference. In December 1931 a British politician crossing Park Avenue in New York City between 76th and 77th Streets around ten-thirty at night looked in the wrong direction and was knocked down by an automobile—a moment, he later recalled, of a man aghast, a world aglare: "I do not understand why I was not broken like an eggshell or squashed like a gooseberry." Fourteen months later an American politician, sitting in an open car in Miami, Florida, was fired on by an assassin; the man beside him was hit. Those who believe that individuals make no difference to history might well ponder whether the next two decades would have been the same had Mario Contasini's car killed Winston Churchill in 1931 and Giuseppe Zangara's bullet killed Franklin Roosevelt in 1933. Suppose, in addition, that Adolf Hitler had been killed in the street fighting during the Munich *Putsch* of 1923 and that Lenin had died of typhus during the First World War. What would the 20th century be like now?

For better or for worse, individuals do make a difference. "The notion that a people can run itself and its affairs anonymously," wrote the philosopher William James, "is now well known to be the silliest of absurdities. Mankind does nothing save through initiatives on the part of inventors, great or small, and imitation by the rest of us—these are the sole factors in human progress. Individuals of genius show the way, and set the patterns, which common people then adopt and follow."

Leadership, James suggests, means leadership in thought as well as in action. In the long run, leaders in thought may well make the greater difference to the world. But, as Woodrow Wilson once said, "Those only are leaders of men, in the general eye, who lead in action. . . . It is at their hands that new thought gets its translation into the crude language of deeds." Leaders in thought often invent in solitude and obscurity, leaving to later generations the tasks of imitation. Leaders in action—the leaders portrayed in this series— have to be effective in their own time.

And they cannot be effective by themselves. They must act in response to the rhythms of their age. Their genius must be adapted, in a phrase of William James's, "to the receptivities of the moment." Leaders are useless without followers. "There goes the mob," said the French politician hearing a clamor in the streets. "I am their leader. I must follow them." Great leaders turn the inchoate emotions of the mob to purposes of their own. They seize on the opportunities of their time, the hopes, fears, frustrations, crises, potentialities.

They succeed when events have prepared the way for them, when the community is waiting to be aroused, when they can provide the clarifying and organizing ideas. Leadership ignites the circuit between the individual and the mass and thereby alters history.

It may alter history for better or for worse. Leaders have been responsible for the most extravagant follies and most monstrous crimes that have beset suffering humanity. They have also been vital in such gains as humanity has made in individual freedom, religious and racial tolerance, social justice and respect for human rights.

There is no sure way to tell in advance who is going to lead for good and who for evil. But a glance at the gallery of men and women in *World Leaders—Past and Present* suggests some useful tests.

One test is this: do leaders lead by force or by persuasion? By command or by consent? Through most of history leadership was exercised by the divine right of authority. The duty of followers was to defer and to obey. "Theirs not to reason why,/ Theirs but to do and die." On occasion, as with the so-called "enlightened despots" of the 18th century in Europe, absolutist leadership was animated by humane purposes. More often, absolutism nourished the passion for domination, land, gold and conquest and resulted in tyranny.

The great revolution of modern times has been the revolution of equality. The idea that all people should be equal in their legal condition has undermined the old structures of authority, hierarchy and deference. The revolution of equality has had two contrary effects on the nature of leadership. For equality, as Alexis de Tocqueville pointed out in his great study *Democracy in America*, might mean equality in servitude as well as equality in freedom.

"I know of only two methods of establishing equality in the political world," Tocqueville wrote. "Rights must be given to every citizen, or none at all to anyone . . . save one, who is the master of all." There was no middle ground "between the sovereignty of all and the absolute power of one man." In his astonishing prediction of 20th-century totalitarian dictatorship, Tocqueville explained how the revolution of equality could lead to the "*Führerprinzip*" and more terrible absolutism than the world had ever known.

But when rights are given to every citizen and the sovereignty of all is established, the problem of leadership takes a new form, becomes more exacting than ever before. It is easy to issue commands and enforce them by the rope and the stake, the concentration camp and the *gulag*. It is much harder to use argument and achievement to overcome opposition and win consent. The Founding Fathers of the United States understood the difficulty. They believed that history had given them the opportunity to decide, as

Alexander Hamilton wrote in the first Federalist Paper, whether men are indeed capable of basing government on "reflection and choice, or whether they are forever destined to depend . . . on accident and force."

Government by reflection and choice called for a new style of leadership and a new quality of followership. It required leaders to be responsive to popular concerns, and it required followers to be active and informed participants in the process. Democracy does not eliminate emotion from politics; sometimes it fosters demagoguery; but it is confident that, as the greatest of democratic leaders put it, you cannot fool all of the people all of the time. It measures leadership by results and retires those who overreach or falter or fail.

It is true that in the long run despots are measured by results too. But they can postpone the day of judgment, sometimes indefinitely, and in the meantime they can do infinite harm. It is also true that democracy is no guarantee of virtue and intelligence in government, for the voice of the people is not necessarily the voice of God. But democracy, by assuring the rights of opposition, offers built-in resistance to the evils inherent in absolutism. As the theologian Reinhold Niebuhr summed it up, "Man's capacity for justice makes democracy possible, but man's inclination to injustice makes democracy necessary."

A second test for leadership is the end for which power is sought. When leaders have as their goal the supremacy of a master race or the promotion of totalitarian revolution or the acquisition and exploitation of colonies or the protection of greed and privilege or the preservation of personal power, it is likely that their leadership will do little to advance the cause of humanity. When their goal is the abolition of slavery, the liberation of women, the enlargement of opportunity for the poor and powerless, the extension of equal rights to racial minorities, the defense of the freedoms of expression and opposition, it is likely that their leadership will increase the sum of human liberty and welfare.

Leaders have done great harm to the world. They have also conferred great benefits. You will find both sorts in this series. Even "good" leaders must be regarded with a certain wariness. Leaders are not demigods; they put on their trousers one leg after another just like ordinary mortals. No leader is infallible, and every leader needs to be reminded of this at regular intervals. Irreverence irritates leaders but is their salvation. Unquestioning submission corrupts leaders and demeans followers. Making a cult of a leader is always a mistake. Fortunately hero worship generates its own antidote. "Every hero," said Emerson, "becomes a bore at last."

The signal benefit the great leaders confer is to embolden the rest of us to live according to our own best selves, to be active, insistent, and resolute in affirming our own sense of things. For great leaders attest to the reality of human freedom against the supposed inevitabilities of history. And they attest to the wisdom and power that may lie within the most unlikely of us, which is why Abraham Lincoln remains the supreme example of great leadership. A great leader, said Emerson, exhibits new possibilities to all humanity. "We feed on genius. . . . Great men exist that there may be greater men."

Great leaders, in short, justify themselves by emancipating and empowering their followers. So humanity struggles to master its destiny, remembering with Alexis de Tocqueville: "It is true that around every man a fatal circle is traced beyond which he cannot pass; but within the wide verge of that circle he is powerful and free; as it is with man, so with communities."

—*New York*

The signal benefit the great leaders confer is to embolden the rest of us to live according to our own best selves, to be active, insistent, and resolute in affirming our own sense of things. For great leaders attest to the reality of human freedom against the supposed inevitabilities of history. And they attest to the wisdom and power that may lie within the most unlikely of us, which is why Abraham Lincoln remains the supreme example of great leadership. A great leader, said Emerson, exhibits new possibilities to all humanity. "We feed on genius. . . . Great men exist that there may be greater men."

Great leaders, in short, justify themselves by emancipating and empowering their followers. So humanity struggles to master its destiny, remembering with Alexis de Tocqueville: "It is true that around every man a fatal circle is traced beyond which he cannot pass; but within the wide verge of that circle he is powerful and free; as it is with man, so with communities."

—*New York*

1

Crown Prince

It was a beautiful horse, bred and broken to battle. The 13-year-old boy stared at it admiringly as his father haggled over its price. His father, Philip, was a veteran soldier, a proud, tough man unused to losing arguments. He also happened to be the king of Macedon. And he was not about to pay so high a price as 13 *talents* without at least testing the horse.

But the steed was in no mood to be ridden that day. Jerking its great head—which had earned it the name Bucephalus, meaning "ox-head"—it reared and snorted and bucked, and none of the riders could mount it. At last they gave up. The horse was too wild, they said. King Philip, having watched their efforts, agreed. "Take the horse away," he bellowed.

The boy had watched in silence, but now he could no longer contain his frustration. Young Alexander was as strong-willed as his father, and he was determined not to lose this fine horse without asserting his personal objections. He insisted that the horse was being rejected only because the riders lacked the courage and skill to handle it.

Understandably, the men laughed, King Philip along with them. Did the child think he knew more about horses than they?

"I think I could handle it better than they have," the boy pleaded. So father and son made a deal. If

There seems to have been some divine hand presiding over both [Alexander's] birth and his actions.
—ARRIAN
second-century Greek historian,
in his *History of Alexander*

Bystanders gape in astonishment as Alexander prepares to subdue the formidable Bucephalus. Horse and boy were only a year apart (Alexander was older), and they were virtually inseparable until Bucephalus died at the age of 29, preceding his master by three years.

Contemporary reports agree that Alexander (356—323 B.C.), with his gray eyes and thick blond hair, was very handsome. Most Macedonian men wore beards, but Alexander, asserting that a beard gave one's enemies a handhold in combat, was clean-shaven. He once ordered his entire army to shave.

Macedon, the beautiful highland kingdom ruled by Alexander's father, King Philip II (382–336 B.C.), lay in territory that today comprises northern Greece and parts of Albania, Yugoslavia, and Bulgaria. Alexander was born at Pella, Macedon's capital.

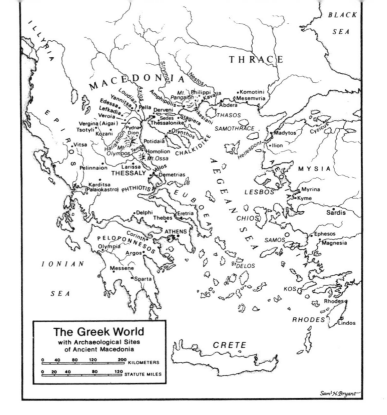

The Greek World
with Archaeological Sites
of Ancient Macedonia

Sam¹H.Bryant

Alexander could mount the fiery Bucephalus, his father would pay for it. If not, the boy would pay for the horse himself.

Alexander ran up to the great black stallion and seized its bridle. As the Roman historian Plutarch tells the story some four centuries later, Alexander had noticed that the horse had seemingly been frightened of its shadow, which for the most part had been in front of it. He swiftly turned the steed toward the sun. Then, "speaking gently to the horse and clapping it on the back with his hand till it had ceased from its fury and snorting," the boy leaped lightly onto its back and galloped it around the field, maintaining such perfect control that boy and animal seemed to move as one.

The men cheered the remarkable feat. Even King Philip, who always drove his son mercilessly, was noticeably impressed. According to Plutarch, Philip fell down weeping for joy and then kissed Alexander's head. "My son," the king said, "you will have to find another kingdom. Macedon is too small for you."

Alexander nodded gravely. Praise from his father was rare. Perhaps the boy took the accolade literally and imagined, if only for a moment this first time, that he might someday enlarge his father's kingdom. Indeed, modesty was not one of young Alexander's most conspicuous virtues.

But even the ambitious Crown Prince Alexander of Macedon might have hesitated to predict for himself the triumphs that were to come. In the 20 years remaining to him, he was to overthrow the great empire of Persia and create another realm, greater by far, stretching from the Balkans to India. Born to be king of Macedon, a small, mountainous kingdom near Greece, he made himself the emperor of Egypt and western Asia by the age of 26.

The boy and the horse were not to part for many years. The Roman historian Curtius wrote that Bucephalus always lowered its huge ox-head to help Alexander mount him, and Arrian, a Greek general in the service of Rome, writing in the 2nd century

The ancient Greek Games, first staged in 776 B.C., were held in Olympia, a religious and political center on the Peloponnese peninsula, now the southern part of modern Greece. Olympian festivals were held on this site for more than a thousand years.

A painted vase depicts Olympic athletes battling it out under the watchful gaze of a referee. Popular in Alexander's day, this event resembled a cross between boxing and wrestling.

A.D., noted that the horse never again allowed anyone but Alexander to ride it. The two became a famous pair. Bucephalus remained capable of great speed for the 17 years during which they were together. When the great horse died in 326 B.C., Alexander built a city, Bucephala, over its grave.

Mastering an unruly horse is not an historic achievement, but it was a sign. Bucephalus knew it instinctively; everyone saw it; even his proud, somewhat jealous father, King Philip, admitted it. Alexander of Macedon was something special.

In fact, something special was expected of Alexander from the day he was born, in 356 B.C. His father, Philip II, was king of a small, backward country just north of Greece. Macedon was a rural land whose people were viewed as semibarbarous by the Greeks. They were allowed to compete in the Greek Festival games—the original Olympics—only because an earlier Macedonian king had made up a story about being descended from the Greek god Heracles. Philip had no hope of raising his country's status except by conquest, and he devoted his life—what remained after drinking and romance—to war. Under him the Macedonians had pushed back the Thracians and the Illyrians—whom even the Macedonians considered barbarians—to the north, and had acquired control over most of the Greek peninsula.

It was while fighting in Thrace that Philip heard the news of his son's birth, which came with two other messages: the Macedonian general Parmenion had won a great battle in Illyria, and Philip's horse had come in first in the Festival races. It was taken to be a good omen for Alexander that his birth coincided with these other victories. In fact the soothsayers assured Philip that these events indicated his son would be invincible.

The 1st-century historian Plutarch reports other early signs—about as convincing. A temple of the goddess Diana had burned down the same night that Alexander was born, proving, for any who cared so to interpret the event, that the goddess had been so busy overseeing the birth that she had not been able to watch over her property. And both of Alexander's parents had dreamed that he would be a great man. His mother, Olympias, was a princess from Epirus, a smaller and more provincial kingdom than Macedon, but she believed herself to be descended from the Greek hero Achilles, and was the high priestess of a woman's religious cult. On the night before her marriage to Philip, she dreamed of a thunderbolt in her womb—proof for her that Alexander was a descendant of the gods.

Apart from all these superstitions, however, there were early personal evidences of Alexander's uniqueness. Ambassadors to Philip's court were astonished at the little boy's intelligence and maturity, and his physical beauty was noted by everyone. He was even said to smell better than others. Plutarch went so far as to report that his body had so sweet a smell that his underwear "took thereof a . . . delightful savor, as if it had been perfumed."

Philip was a sensualist, a lover of physical pleasure. Half-Illyrian himself, he inherited some of the

Achilles, the legendary Greek warrior who was the hero of Homer's epic poem the *Iliad*, gets an archery lesson from Chiron, the wise centaur (a mythical hybrid of man and horse) who tutored him. The family of Alexander's mother, Olympias (d. 316 B.C.), claimed to be descended from Achilles.

Dionysus, the Greek god of wine and fertility, inspires a riotous celebration similar to the kinds of uninhibited activity that Philip of Macedon enjoyed. His son, Alexander, was far more straight laced.

wild, primitive traits of that tribe, whose present-day descendants, the Albanians, claim Alexander as their own. Philip was a great fighter who revolutionized the art of war. But he had a weakness for wine and women, which finally proved his undoing. Alexander was quite different. He inherited little of that taste for liquor and love, and was known for his composure and chastity even as a youth.

One thing he did share with his father was a fierce independence. The two often clashed, and while the rough warrior Philip was proud of his son and clearly thought of him as his heir, he often found him puzzling. Olympias repeatedly insisted that the boy's real father was a god. Perhaps Philip came to suspect that, if Alexander's father was not necessarily divine, he might not have been King Philip, either. Whatever the reasons, Philip soon cooled to Olympias and began to find his pleasures elsewhere.

Infidelity Philip could have understood, engaging in it as freely as he did himself, but his wife's mean temper and cold religious spirit (not to mention the tame snakes she kept in her bedroom as part of her religious cult) were incomprehensible and repulsive to him. Alexander seemed to have taken after her side of the family in some ways. Philip could identify with his son's skill and daring, but the boy's seriousness seemed unnatural. Alexander did not seem to want what most other boys wanted. He did not indulge himself in drink or sex or fun.

The only thing Alexander wanted was to accomplish great things. His dedication to achievement was obsessive. Even as a child he once cried out, after his father had overrun some city, "My father will have everything, and I will have nothing left to conquer!"

He knew he was to be a king, and never saw himself as anything less. There is a story that when he was invited to compete in the Festival Games—he was already a notable runner—he refused. It was not appropriate, he said, to run against commoners. He would participate only if he could compete with kings.

At age seven a Macedonian boy was expected to be ready for formal study, and Philip appointed a severe tutor, Leonidas, to guide his son's scholastic progress. Leonidas was noted for advocating lean diet and strenuous exercise, and Alexander duly submitted to this regime, though probably without much enthusiasm. Philip could see that under Leonidas's tutelage Alexander was being prepared for the battlefield more than for the throne. A night march to make him want his breakfast, and a small breakfast to make him hungry for supper may have hardened the boy's small, tough body, but it did little for his mind, and Philip wanted a well-rounded training for his son and heir. He began looking for the best available tutor, and, when Alexander reached age 13, selected the son of a former court physician to the Macedonian kings. His name was Aristotle.

This Greek philosopher, then in his early 40s, was not yet the legendary figure he was to become, but as a student of the celebrated Plato he had admirable credentials. Philip paid him well and gave him a pleasant little villa in the quiet town of Mieza near the Macedonian capital of Pella. There Aristotle nourished Alexander's intellectual development for approximately three years.

A painted vase depicts a 6th-century B.C. footrace. Alexander loved strenuous exercise like hunting, running, and ball games, but he was too proud to participate in competitive athletics, fearing that he might be named a winner because of his royal blood.

Plato (427–347 B.C.), the Greek philosopher who was Aristotle's teacher, founded a school called the Academy in 387 B.C., in Athens. The world's first university, it flourished for almost 800 years. Plato's most famous work, the *Republic*, deals with the nature of ideal government and proposes that such government might best be achieved by a ruling class of philosopher-kings.

Homer is believed to have been the author of the *Iliad* and the *Odyssey*, epic poems about the Trojan War and the wanderings of Odysseus, or Ulysses. Indisputable facts about Homer, however, are few; historians have placed his birth anywhere from 850 to 1200 B.C.

The choice was a fateful one, and was to influence the history of the world. The two hit it off at once, the contemplative, middle-aged philosopher and the bright, ever-curious Macedonian lad. Aristotle immediately set about correcting the crude Macedonian dialect of his royal charge. He also inspired in him a love of Greek literature, as well as a sense of scientific method and a regard for logic. The boy soon developed an appreciation of the great dramatists of Greece. His reverence for the works of the poet Pindar was revealed years later when, upon destroying the city of Thebes, he left the poet's home untouched. Above all, however, he devoured the *Iliad*, Homer's great epic poem about Greece's war against Troy. This was a pivotal book in Alexander's education, and from it he absorbed many Greek values and ideas. In fact, he slept with it—along with a dagger—under his pillow every night for the rest of his life.

A love of literature, however, was not the most important thing Aristotle gave Alexander, though it definitely influenced everything else. Even more important were Aristotle's efforts in training the heir-apparent for kingship. Plato's dream had been a world ruled by philosopher-kings, and it is almost certain that his disciple Aristotle must have seen in the sensitive, intelligent young prince a partial promise of that great dream's fulfillment.

The teacher-pupil relationship came to an abrupt end in 340 B.C. In that year, the 16-year-old prince was summoned back to Pella to serve as king while his father was fighting at Byzantium, in southern Thrace.

It was a great trust and included custody of the royal seal of Macedon, which gave official approval to all government documents. Some of the nobles in the court thought it was too much to ask of a 16-year-old boy still learning grammar and arithmetic. But Alexander of Macedon was no ordinary 16-year-old. He performed his new duties effectively and kept a watchful eye over his father's interests. It was his first taste of real power, and he took to it as if he had been ruling all his life.

The leading Greek thinker Aristotle (384–322 B.C.), whose interests ranged from philosophy and poetry to medicine and science, instructs Alexander. The future king was especially fascinated by botany and zoology. In later years, he sent Aristotle animal and plant specimens that he had collected on his military campaigns.

2

Soldier

Within the year, Alexander had the chance to try on not only his father's crown but his war helmet as well. The Maedi, a Thracian tribe subject to the Macedonians, took advantage of Philip's absence to rebel, and the young Alexander had his first chance at military command. The soldiers accepted the boy's orders and obediently followed him into the hills of what is now Bulgaria, where they made short work of the half-savage rebels. Then, like his father, Alexander established a Macedonian stronghold by founding a city: Alexandropolis, the City of Alexander. This small city, the first of the many that were to bear his name, has long since disappeared. While Alexander's first experience of command involved little more than suppressing a minor rebellion, its successful outcome must have awakened the appetite for glory that was to characterize him throughout his life. In the meantime, his father was fighting on a much larger scale, and for much bigger stakes.

Since long before Alexander's birth, Philip had been expanding the boundaries of his kingdom, and had subdued one after another of the independent Greek city-states that dared to oppose him. Considered by some historians to have been the first modern military leader, he undoubtedly cre-

The bronze war helmet worn by properly equipped Greek soldiers was elaborately decorated with gold and silver inlays, and topped by a horsehair crest dyed in brilliant colors.

Even in full battle regalia, an infantryman in the Macedonian army was lightly armed in comparison to warriors of later eras. Carrying a sword, he was protected only by his engraved bronze shield, helmet, breastplate, and greaves, or leg armor.

Macedonian support troops prepare for battle. Even today, military historians are dazzled by Philip's masterful use of cavalrymen and sword-armed warriors on the flanks, while he deployed the phalanx as a solid center line against the enemy. Such tactics earned his small but well-forged army a string of impressive victories.

ated an army that was exceptionally organized and professional by the standards of those times. Drilled, trained, and disciplined much like the armies of today, Philip's soldiers swept all before them. By the time Alexander fought among them, they threatened even Athens. This great metropolis was the most powerful and influential of all the city-states and the greatest cultural center in all Greece.

Some Athenians wanted peace and unity, and hoped that Philip would take over. They had a vision of the entire Greek peninsula becoming a Hellenic (Greek) nation, united under a single government. Such a powerful political entity, they thought, could protect itself against the ever-threatening barbarians and perhaps even expand the range of Greek power. Some shared Philip's dream of attacking the great Persian Empire to the east and adding the Greek colonies there to the land within their own boundaries.

But most Athenians saw Philip as a threat to their cherished independence. Demosthenes, the most famous of all Greek orators, spoke against

Philip in a series of three speeches, so violent and bitter that the word "Philippic" survives in English to describe any biting verbal attack.

In fact, Demosthenes was so persuasive with his Philippics that the Athenians rallied to fight against "the Barbarian of the North." To defend their independence they allied themselves with Thebes, the principal city of Boeotia, and the second city of all Greece. The Athenians were famous as scholars, artists, and thinkers, while the Thebans were renowned as soldiers. The Theban "Sacred Band," an elite 300-man troop dedicated to the art of war, was considered unbeatable. Together, the Athenians and the Thebans believed, they could surely crush the upstart Philip.

But the king of Macedon, using his knowledge of military tactics gained while serving as a hostage in Thebes years before, had gradually built up an army that had all the advantages of the Theban band—unity, dedication, discipline, and strategic prowess—plus one thing more. It had Alexander.

Philip was well pleased with the boy's conduct of operations against the Maedi. Everything the king had learned of strategy and leadership, both in the classroom and on the battlefield, he had passed on to his son. The young crown prince was a seasoned soldier now, and at age 18 was ready for the responsibility of high command. Philip made Alexan-

A mercenary soldier signs up with the Athenian army. By the time Philip came into direct confrontation with Athens, in 338 B.C., the city-state was finding it increasingly difficult to recruit its own citizens, and had begun to accept political refugees, soldiers of fortune, and even slaves for military service.

The Parthenon, ravaged by wars and weather for 24 centuries but still standing today, was exactly 100 years old when Philip beat the Athenian army in 338 B.C. Built to honor Athena, the Greek goddess for whom the city-state was named, the majestic temple is regarded as one of the architectural wonders of the world.

der a general in the Macedonian army and called him to the field in Chaeronea.

The battle of Chaeronea, fought on the plains of northern Greece, was the decisive engagement in Philip's war with the Greeks. Athens had prepared for a major confrontation, supported by the Theban army. Defeat here for Philip would have meant the end of his ambitions; victory promised control of all Greece.

Philip set the scene himself. Knowing that Athenian power lay principally in naval strength, he arranged for a false military dispatch to be intercepted, and drew the combined forces of Athens and Thebes to an inland battleground. At dawn on August 4, 338 B.C., he attacked.

Thirty thousand Athenian and Theban infantrymen faced an equal number of Macedonians. Philip's

Philip found you as poor nomads, clothed in sheepskin while you pastured your sparse sheep in the mountains. He gave you cloaks instead of skins, brought you down from the mountains and gave you cities; civilized you with good laws and customs.
—ALEXANDER
rallying mutinous troops
late in his career

forces were composed of cavalry and a *phalanx*—foot soldiers tightly drawn together in parallel ranks, almost shoulder to shoulder. *Phalanx* is the Greek word for "finger," and this deep column could prod and jab like a long, vicious finger into the enemy lines. The phalanx was invented in Thebes, but Philip had improved on the Theban version. He had increased the number of lines and armed his men with giant, 15-foot-long spears, the famous "Macedonian lances." The Theban phalanx hurled its nine-foot spears and depended on fresh supplies from behind, but the Macedonian lances were

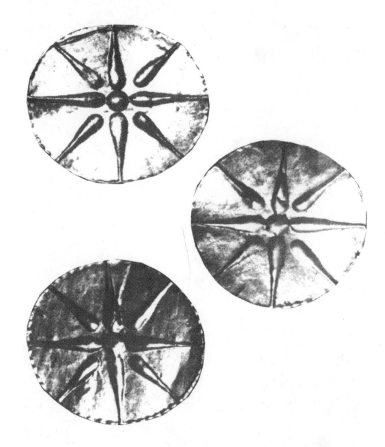

A starburst, the royal Macedonian emblem, is embossed on gold discs uncovered by archeologists in a royal burial chamber in 1977. The tomb had been untouched for more than 2,300 years.

gripped and thrust, and no one could get near the men who held them. Philip selected tough, strong men of uniform height to produce a compact, impregnable mass. He used the phalanx as a defensive force and the cavalry for attacking.

The Athenians drove in on the Macedonian phalanx, and to their delight saw it fall back. They raced on in pursuit, sure of victory, until their lines were thinned almost to the breaking point— just as Philip had planned. His phalanx wheeled around and scattered the Athenian infantry. Then the Macedonian cavalry, led by the 18-year-old Alexander, charged the Theban forces on the other side of the battlefield. Alexander's 2,000 mounted soldiers fought fiercely, chopping the Thebans down until none remained but the Sacred Band, sworn to die rather than submit. And die they did. Of the 300 soldiers who made up this select force, only 46 were captured. The rest fought till they dropped. By noon, King Philip of Macedon had become the chief power in Greece.

But Philip did not want to be king of Greece. In fact, he made very generous terms with his defeated enemy. He took no revenge against Athens, released all Athenian prisoners without asking for ransom, and left the city its Aegean islands. With Thebes, however, he was more stern. Recognizing the threat Thebes could become, he dissolved the alliance (the Boeotian League) it had formed with other cities in its province. He also garrisoned the city with Macedonian troops.

All he asked for himself was the command of a unified Greek army, supported by all the Hellenic city-states, for his march against Persia. This had

Columns in the form of sculptured female figures support the roof of the Erechtheum, a temple that remains one of Athens's most breathtaking sights after almost 2,400 years. The Erechtheum stands on the Acropolis, where the Athenians erected statues of Philip and Alexander after the Macedonian victory at Chaeronea in 338 B.C.

The mighty Macedonian phalanx annihilates the Thracian army in 335 B.C. Alexander had improved on the military techniques he learned from his father; even more important, he had the unquestioning trust of his dedicated troops. "While I have led you," he told them, "not one of you has been killed in flight."

been the dream of his life, the ambition which gave real purpose to his conquests in Greece.

Philip's ultimate goal was the destruction of the Persian Empire. He saw it as a holy crusade and a just punishment for earlier Persian conquests in Greece. Victory over the Persians would unify Greece and provide a rich source of loot for the Greek treasury. And there would be support from within Persia, too. Many provinces in the Persian Empire were unhappy, and the Greek colonies under Persian rule would welcome their liberation.

Athens, relieved that Philip had proven so lenient a conqueror, voted to support his plan. Soon the other city-states fell into line—all except Sparta, which never submitted to Macedon. At Corinth, a league of Hellenic cities was established. They remained independent, but under the central control of the panhellenic (united Greek) army of Philip of Macedon. This federation, known as the League of Corinth, was to become the master of the known world.

A medallion shows a muscular Spartan warrior, protected only by his shield and sword. Every able-bodied Spartan citizen belonged to the army of the state, which guarded its independence by remaining on perpetual war-alert.

Sparta's open market served as a center for social and business exchange among the people of the fiercely independent city-state. Plato's *Republic* was partially influenced by his observations on the Spartan system of government, which legislated sexual equality and state control of property, industry, education, and morals.

3

King

> *The King is changed only in name, and the State will be run on principles no less effective than those of my father.*
> —ALEXANDER
> speaking in 336 B.C.

Philip, at age 45, was at the high point of his life. At last he held the power he had fought for. Philip had imposed peace—albeit a tense, uncertain peace —throughout the Greek peninsula. However, things were not so harmonious at home.

Philip and Olympias had long been estranged, and in 337 B.C. the King's eye strayed to a pretty young girl in his court. She was the niece of the powerful noble Attalus. Philip had had enough of his wife's cold, superior ways and her pet snakes, and he decided to divorce her and marry his new favorite.

Macedonian law permitted him to marry as many women as he wanted, but only one could be queen. His decision changed everything for Olympias. She may not have cared much for Philip by this time, if she ever had, but her pride as woman, wife, and queen was stung. In the past Olympias had swallowed Philip's love affairs, but to be turned out of her royal palace for a girl younger than their own child was too much. She was furious, and Alexander, who had not been getting along with his father to begin with, sided entirely with her. In his eyes it was not only an indignity and an insult to the family, it was a serious threat to the ambitious young prince's prospect of inheriting the throne of

---

A 19th-century engraving shows Alexander as a romantic hero triumphing over a serpent, symbol of evil in both pagan and Christian folklore. In the centuries since his death, the Macedonian king has inspired legends, poems, and paintings in almost every country in the world.

Philip's imposing features were recorded by a contemporary sculptor in a miniature but powerfully executed ivory carving. Alexander's father was not always as serious as he looked; he is said to have been the first barbershop customer who responded to the question, "How would you like your hair cut, sir?" by saying, "In silence."

A Greek theatrical mask found in the ruins of the Roman city of Pompeii. Drama was part of everyday life in ancient Greece, and no important event took place without a theatrical performance. Philip was about to watch a play celebrating his daughter's wedding when he was murdered.

Macedon. Olympias was, after all, an Epirote—a barbarian—while Philip's new wife was of a high-ranking, pure Macedonian family. If Philip had a son with his new wife, the son of the foreigner Olympias might have a problem proving his right to succeed Philip as king.

And as if this point were not clear enough to him, the wedding party made it clearer. The girl's uncle, Attalus, a little too drunk for good sense, toasted the newlyweds with the tactless hope that they would produce a legitimate heir to the crown.

That was the last straw for Alexander. He threw a cup at the old man's head and shouted, "What am I, then? A bastard?" The king, probably drunker than either, jumped up and drew his sword. He lurched toward his son, but collapsed in the middle of the room. "Look at that!" sneered Alexander. "He is planning to march from Europe into Asia and he cannot make it from one couch to another."

With that, he and his mother left the court and the country. For several months Alexander stayed away. Olympias went to Epirus, her brother's kingdom, and Alexander settled in Illyria, where the harsh climate and the primitive lifestyle of his former enemies suited his angry mood. Philip was

unhappy about the situation but refused to take the first step to patch things up with his son. At last a diplomat from Corinth convinced Philip that it looked ridiculous for him to keep talking about unity among the Greeks when he could not even keep his own family together. The king grudgingly invited his son back.

Alexander returned but with no great affection, and the family lived together in a sort of armed truce. It was a tense household. In the first place, Alexander resented his new, young stepmother. And over the border to the west, Olympias's brother, the king of Epirus, remained furious at the insult to his sister.

To placate his brother-in-law Philip made what seems today a strange offer. He would give his own daughter as a wife. Marriage between uncle and niece was not uncommon in those days, especially in royal families, and the king of Epirus had no objection to his sister's daughter as a bride. In fact, he was delighted to once again be linked by marriage with the royal house of Macedon. How Olympias—or Alexander—felt about it is not recorded.

Philip immediately set about planning the most

An ancient Greek vase shows women weaving, dyeing, and folding woolen cloth. Regarded as a subspecies, like slaves and barbarians (non-Greeks), women were valued in Greek society only for their abilities to work and bear sons. Even the learned Aristotle taught that woman was an "imperfect" form of man.

Alexander and Olympias. Although mother and son bore a strong resemblance to each other, father and son did not. Alexander was very young when Olympias hinted that his real father was the god Zeus, an idea he never completely forgot.

lavish wedding in history. It would show everyone both how peaceful his family relations now were and how substantial was his wealth. To add to the drama, Philip's young bride gave birth to a boy during the preparations—a cause of great dismay to Alexander, whose claim on the title of heir apparent was greatly weakened. Things were coming to a head in the royal house of Macedon.

But the real climax of the mounting domestic crisis was something no one could have foreseen. On the day of the wedding, in the midst of the final procession, a young Macedonian noble in Philip's personal bodyguard pulled a short sword from under his cloak and stabbed the king through the heart, killing him instantly.

The crime had nothing to do with politics or family or inheritance of the throne. It was a strictly personal affair. The assassin had been humiliated by Attalus, the uncle of Philip's new wife, and had received no satisfaction from the king when he complained about it. That he was encouraged by Olympias seems quite likely, but it could never be proved, since the young noble was killed as he tried to escape.

Immediately after the murder Alexander, with that calm assurance that was always his most striking characteristic, announced that he was king. The army, with whom he had been popular since his first campaign, accepted him without question.

But other voices soon made themselves heard, and Alexander knew they had to be stilled. Attalus was quick to point out that his niece's infant son by Philip had a clearer claim to the crown. Alexander lost no time in settling that claim. He sent a trusted soldier to arrest Attalus or kill him, whichever proved easier, and the messenger understood the order. As a general, Attalus was too dangerous to leave alive.

Olympias was more direct in her response. After crowning the killer, she set about disposing of any possible claimant to her son's title. Historians differ about her treatment of Philip's young wife and child. The kindest and most probable version is that she forced Cleopatra to hang herself after watch-

Philip dies by the sword, 336 B.C. Some accounts say the assassin's blade struck the king's heart, others that he was stabbed in the back, but there is no doubt that he died on the spot.

Herodotus, a Greek historian of the 5th century B.C., is known as the "Father of History" because of his highly polished account of the wars between Greece and Persia from 500 to 479 B.C. Both Philip and Alexander were determined to avenge the defeats that Greece had suffered during this protracted conflict.

ing the death of her baby. Another account has her dragging them both over a bronze container full of burning coals, and a third says that she had them boiled alive. She may not have done any of these things, but she was evidently the sort of woman who inspired such stories.

Between Olympias's personal ferocity and her son's cool, methodical legality, most of the threats to his position were removed at once. Philip's nephew had as good a claim as Alexander, but he was duly tried and executed for conspiracy. So were two princes of a family that had earlier claimed the right to kingship. In a matter of months, Alexander's title as king of Macedon was unopposed except by Demosthenes, who, once he stopped applauding the murder of the father, turned his hatred on the

A mask of Silenus, an ancient Greek god of the forest; he was foster father and companion of Dionysus, the god of fertility and wine. Olympias was a lifelong member of a Dionysian cult whose rites often culminated in animal or human sacrifice.

The ruins of the Hall of Votive Gifts, a 6th-century B.C. temple on the island of Samothrace. Philip had first met Olympias here, during a celebration of the mysteries of the Cabiri, twin gods who were believed to promote fertility and to protect their worshipers from shipwreck.

son. The orator never relented in his opposition to Macedonian control of Athens. But Demosthenes could say what he liked. It changed nothing. At age 20 Alexander was king.

He inherited a loyal country with a devoted army. He also inherited a mission. Philip had forced a sort of unity on Greece and had had himself made commander-in-chief of its army. Now his son, Alexander III, king of Macedon, set about establishing his worthiness to that title as well. His father had started a war of revenge against Persia, to retake the lands which that great empire had conquered from Greece a century before. But Alexander had higher aspirations, and a higher destiny. He would go beyond his father's dream and surpass his triumphs. He would conquer the world.

Alexander considered that he had come from the gods to be a general governor and reconciler of the world. Using force of arms when he did not bring men together by the light of reason, he harnessed all resources to one and the same end, mixing the lives, manners, marriages and customs of men, as it were in a loving-cup.
—PLUTARCH
Greek historian (A.D. 46–120), in his *Lives of the Noble Grecians and Romans*

Alexander, both during his lifetime and for many centuries afterward, inspired countless portraits. His likeness was especially popular with the Romans. When the supply of original pieces was exhausted, they commissioned sculptors to produce copies.

4

Commander-in-Chief

Alexander's first objective as king was to strengthen his shaky position at home. Executing potential enemies at court was not enough. He needed a vote of confidence.

It was obvious from the start that Alexander did not have universal support. Philip's old enemies in Athens saw a chance to repudiate the agreement they had made to support Macedonia in a war against Persia, and Demosthenes (who was suspected of having financed the assassination) openly wore a triumphal garland of flowers on his head before the Athenian assembly. Thessaly, a city-state which had never been firm in its support of Philip, and certainly had no loyalty to his son, proclaimed its independence at once, as did Sparta. The League of Corinth was falling apart. Alexander had no sure friends in Greece.

His first order of business was Thessaly, in the south. Before the Thessalians could prepare for battle, Alexander quickly put himself at the head of his army and marched into the region with 30,000 men. The Thessalians were so shocked they offered no resistance and surrendered without a sword being drawn. It was a promising start for Alexander.

With this easy victory behind him, he turned his attention to reunifying and gaining the official support of the League of Corinth. He had inherited his

Demosthenes, white-robed and wreathed, urges his fellow citizens to give thanks for the joyful news of Philip's murder, and to reject the rule of Alexander. The acid-tongued orator convinced the Athenians that the young Alexander was a "simpleton," a judgment they later revised.

Astride the mighty Bucephalus, Alexander leads his men to victory over the rebellious Thessalians. He accomplished his bloodless coup with a semicircular advance: As the rebels awaited his army's appearance from the north, it suddenly appeared behind them. Stunned, they surrendered at once.

father's kingdom and army, and now he wanted backing from the rest of Greece. Since he already commanded the strongest army in the peninsula, the league had no real alternative but to endorse him. Sparta, once again, was the exception.

Alexander received the congratulations of many famous people at Corinth, but one he particularly wanted to meet was Diogenes the Cynic, a great philosopher of the time and the most famous citizen of Corinth. He was known to sleep in a tub and always carried a lit lantern during the day, explaining that he was looking for an honest man.

Alexander was anxious to see this respected eccentric and sought him out in the suburb where he lived. The old man was sitting in front of his tub sunning himself. He ignored Alexander's greeting completely, but the king persisted. "Is there anything I can do for you?" he asked the philosopher at last. "Yes," replied Diogenes, "You can move aside. You are keeping the sun off me."

The incident has been often quoted. Certainly, it was one of the few occasions upon which Alexander the Great ever received a personal slight to his

Diogenes (412—323 B.C.) carries his famous lantern in search of honesty. A believer in a community of all mankind rather than of small separate states, Diogenes coined the word "cosmopolite," meaning "citizen of the world." This concept became increasingly meaningful as Alexander's campaigns of conquest extended the boundaries of the known world.

face, and it impressed him. "By Zeus," he is reported to have exclaimed later, "if I were not Alexander, I would like to be Diogenes!"

But he had little time now for philosophical speculations. He had determined on a march to the Danube River, and he turned his men northward. He expected little opposition along the way, although he knew he had to pass through hostile Thracian territory in the Balkans. But in a narrow pass in those mountains the Macedonian troops found the local tribesmen ready to fight.

These fierce warriors, who took enemy heads as souvenirs of their battles, had fortified the rocky pass heavily and lined its upper slopes with many heavy wagons. Alexander, who had fought them before, anticipated their plan: as soon as the Macedonian phalanx came within range, the Thracians would push the wagons so that they would roll down the slope and crush the tightly massed troops below. Then they would rush in and fight the remaining Macedonians hand to hand.

Acting quickly, Alexander directed his men to open up the phalanx to let the cars pass through. Those who could not get out of the way were in-

Alexander's orders to his troops, which saved them from a Thracian ambush in this Balkan pass in 335 B.C., were followed with the precision of a parade-field drill. Not a man was lost, proving once again that the army Alexander had inherited from Philip was the finest in the world.

Alexander thought it more worthy of a king to conquer his own emotions than an enemy.
—PLUTARCH

Their plan to crush the Macedonians thwarted, Thracian warriors make a futile stand. The lightly armed defenders were no match for Alexander's invincible phalanx; 1,500 Thracians soon lay dead on the field.

structed to throw themselves flat on the ground and cover themselves with their large shields. The wagons passed harmlessly over their bodies. The only weapons the Thracians had were light javelins and daggers, and they had little protection. The Macedonians cut them to pieces and captured the pass.

At last the way was clear to the mighty Danube, a river none had yet been able to cross because of the powerful tribes that defended its banks. There was no particular tactical reason to cross it, except perhaps to show the local tribes that Macedonians could do anything they set out to do. As historian Mary Renault points out, Alexander wanted to make an impression on the Getae who held the opposite bank. "If he crossed to their side," she writes, "they might later feel discouraged from crossing to his."

The Macedonians had no boats, and the Danube is a wide river. But once Alexander seized upon an idea, he allowed nothing to stand in his way. His urge to cross the Danube—to triumph over this natural obstacle as he had triumphed over so many personal obstacles—was irresistible. He ordered the army's tent-skins to be stuffed with hay and tied together, and on these improvised rafts he ferried his 5,000 troops across the river during the night without losing a single man.

Once on the other side, in present-day Romania, the Macedonians hid in the tall grass until dawn. The Getae were so startled when they finally saw them that they fled in terror. The plunder left behind was the Macedonians' only tangible reward for the adventure. For Alexander, however, the triumph was symbolically rich.

By now the might and tactical abilities of the Macedonian army was known far and wide. Tribes from all along the river began to send representatives to offer their allegiance to the invincible Alexander. The tall Celts—a widely dispersed people who occupied parts of present-day France and England as well as central Europe—swore to fight faithfully for him, as did many other tribes. By the time Alexander had floated his army back across the Danube, the propaganda value of the exploit had paid off handsomely. The Macedonian army inspired respect and fear everywhere, and Alexander felt sure that the march to Asia would be easy.

Two types of helmet worn by Macedonian *hoplites*, or foot soldiers. The solid bronze helmets' original components, now lost, included leather nose-guards and cheek protectors.

The bone-chilling, almost supernatural sight of Alexander's phalanx drilling in full battle dress—and absolute silence — unnerved the usually fearless Illyrians, and paved the way for yet another Macedonian victory.

Alexander's assault drove the panicked Theban defenders back into the city from their positions outside its walls. Their failure to close the gates behind them allowed the Macedonians to stream into the fortified city, where thousands of civilians died in the fierce street fighting that followed.

But at home all was not peace and harmony. No sooner did Alexander get his men on the march than he learned that three Illyrian tribes had once again risen in revolt and joined forces along the western border of Macedonia. There they planned to intercept Alexander's army during its return through what is now Yugoslavia. The Illyrians did not have the military polish of the Macedonian army, but they were powerful warriors, especially on their own terrain. After sacrificing six children to their war gods, they were ready to avenge all the defeats they had suffered over the years at the hands of Alexander and his father.

By all the laws of logic, Macedonian history should have ended right there on the plains of Illyria. Alexander's troops were weary from a hard fight and a long march, and they faced a savage band that outnumbered them three to one. But the Macedonian king was always able to devise a military strategy appropriate for a given situation. This time he relied on the superstitious fear that he inspired in his enemies. He ordered his men to do close-order drills in total silence, almost as if celebrating some religious ceremony. In full view of the Illyrians, a tight, 120-man-deep phalanx paraded noiselessly up and down the plain. The Illyrian tribesmen had never seen anything like it. They watched in bewilderment, slowly moving closer. Then Alexander gave his signal.

At once, his men moved into place and charged, every soldier beating his spear on his shield and shouting the Macedonian war cry. The sudden and thunderous outburst terrified the Illyrians, who dropped their swords and scurried away like rats. In a moment the Macedonian cavalry was upon them, chopping them to the ground before they could catch their breaths. The catapults and bowmen finished what the cavalry and infantry had begun. Again the Macedonian army escaped without the loss of a single soldier.

That night the Macedonians marched in force to the Illyrian camp and cut down any who had taken refuge there. Those who were sleeping never awoke. Those who struggled to escape were killed before they could pick up arms. The massacre put an end once and for all to Illyrian opposition. Once again Alexander prevailed.

On those occasions when the military situation demanded it, Alexander could rely not only upon his superbly disciplined troops, but also upon his artillery, which included siege machines capable of hurling a 50-pound rock 500 feet. The Macedonian army also included personnel with medical training: a private physician for Alexander and another to tend his warriors.

On his way home from Thebes, Alexander visited the temple of the Delphic oracle (priestess) to find out if his Persian campaign would succeed. The oracle, claiming it was an unlucky day, declined to speak, but Alexander grabbed her by the hair and insisted. "My son," she said at last, "you are invincible."

A Macedonian officer meets his death at the hands of Timoclea, the widow of a Theban general. Brought before Alexander, Timoclea defiantly admitted pushing the officer down a well after he had raped her. Alexander, impressed by her audacity, ordered Timoclea and her children freed.

> After each battle Alexander went to see the wounded, looking at their wounds, asking how they got them, encouraging each to tell about his deeds and even brag of them.
>
> —ARRIAN

One last confrontation remained to him in Greece. Demosthenes, seizing upon Alexander's long absence, had roused the Thebans to revolt. They had lost the Sacred Band to Macedon's long spears at Chaeronea, but they were still a potent fighting force, and despite the Macedonian garrison that was stationed there they declared their independence of Alexander's rule.

To strengthen his case, Demosthenes invented the story that Alexander and all his army had been killed in the fighting to the north. He even produced a bogus eyewitness to the supposed event. When Alexander heard the news, he sent word to the Thebans that he was indeed alive and well and would tolerate no defection.

Some of the Thebans backed down at once. Others argued that they could stage a successful fight against the battle-weary Macedonian troops. At last, the city voted to fight for freedom.

As Alexander neared the gates of Thebes he sent word that he would give them one last chance. Any who wanted could leave the city and join his ranks.

He also promised that if the leaders of the revolt were handed over to him, he would pardon the rest.

The Theban reply was defiant: any who wanted to join Thebes in freeing the Greeks from the tyranny of Macedon could come over to *them*. This infuriated Alexander. He determined that Thebes, that ancient, historic city, must be destroyed utterly as an example and a warning to the rest of Greece.

And destroy it he did. Once again the long lances and superior fighting skills of Macedon carried the day. Infants, old women, priests, and invalids alike were put to the sword. Only the house of Pindar, the ancient poet Alexander had admired since his student days with Aristotle, was spared. Six thousand Thebans were butchered, and all the rest taken as slaves. Theban exiles were banished from Greece, and the city was completely razed. Thebes was no more.

> *We will keep faith unless the sky fall and crush us, or the earth open and swallow us, or the sea rise and overwhelm us.*
> —Celtic oath of loyalty to Alexander, 335 B.C.

In the ghastly hush pervading Thebes after its downfall, Alexander sentences Theban captives. The 20,000 citizens who survived the Macedonian attack—when "every corner was piled high with corpses," according to an observer— were sold into slavery.

5

Invader

A moving world was his camp. ... The market that followed him was like a capital city's; anything could be bought there, were it as rare as bird's milk.
—anonymous Persian chronicler

As the commander of the panhellenic army, Alexander was ready now to carry out his mission. We can not know how far his ambitions reached at this point—whether he wanted only to finish his father's task of freeing the Greek colonies in Asia Minor (present-day Turkey) and restoring them to Greece, or whether he already dreamed of toppling the Persian empire. We do know that he made preparations at once to march east.

The army he assembled numbered some 30,000 infantry and 5,000 cavalry—a small force to conquer an empire. But it was not as rash as many historians have suggested. Centuries of peace had weakened the Persian fighting forces, and the empire was deeply divided politically. Alexander also knew he could depend on support from many of the subject tribes under Persian rule once he presented himself to them as a liberator.

And he knew that the Macedonian phalanx was the most powerful military machine the world had ever seen. Disciplined, dedicated, brave, and flexible, Alexander's army had never lost a battle, and its enthusiasm about the coming campaign was great.

Still, Alexander knew this was to be no easy victory. He was not attacking some forest tribe of barbarians, tattooed and dressed in fox skins, like the Thracians. The Persian empire was a vast and ancient one, with a culture as old and as advanced

A **Phoenician seaman.** The Persians' strongest military branch was their navy, which boasted 400 warships, built and manned largely by sailors from Phoenicia, a seacoast nation in the region of present-day Syria, Lebanon, and Israel.

In the first of their three great battles, Macedonians and Persians meet at the Granicus River. This was Darius's (d. 330 B.C.) supreme opportunity to drive Alexander from the Persian Empire once and for all, but through mismanagement and overconfidence, he lost his chance. He would never have another.

Greeted as a liberator, Alexander enters a Persian coastal city. The Macedonian avoided sea battles in his conquest of Persia; he knew the Persians' Phoenician seamen were more experienced than his own, and furthermore, he had seen an eagle on the shore, a sign that he should seek victory on land rather than at sea.

as that of Greece. It was the most powerful the East had ever known. One of its kings, Darius I, had conquered Thrace and Macedon in the sixth century B.C., and in the fifth century, another, Xerxes, had sacked Athens. Their present ruler, "The Great King" Darius III, Lord of Asia, was said to have a million men ready to be put into the field in case of attack. The army may have become soft through years of inactivity, but it was still a huge and potent force, in a land of almost limitless resources. In the century and a half since the Persians had looted and burned Athens, they had had no one to fear, and this semibarbarian youth from Macedon did not alarm the Great King unduly.

Alexander placed his father's old general Antipater on the throne of Macedon as his regent, said goodbye to his mother, and set out with his small Athenian fleet in the spring of 334 B.C. for the Hellespont—the juncture of West and East.

There is a story that when his boat approached the Asian shore, he hurled his javelin onto the land as a token that he intended to take the continent. The action certainly would have been in keeping with his youthful confidence.

And in fact he saw no reason to doubt his success. The Persian fleet—actually the great Phoenician navy, the best and strongest in the world and three times as large as Alexander's—smugly ignored his crossing into Asia, confident that the Persians could deal with him easily enough on the land. This was, as historian Peter Green observes in his *Alexander the Great*, "the most extraordinary piece of good luck for Alexander. . . . A determined attack by sea during the actual crossing might well have scotched the invasion before it was well launched." Alexander's first action, once on shore, was to visit Ilium, the ancient Troy, in what is now Turkey. Here, nine centuries before, Greece's first invasion of Asia had taken place, and the Trojan War still lay deep in the national memory of the Greeks. It was the subject of their great epic, the *Iliad*, the book Alexander kept underneath his pillow every night. A visit to this sacred place was like a religious pilgrimage to him. It was, after all, from Achilles, a hero in that war, that he traced his own descent and it was this almost invincible warrior that he looked to all his life for a model. Now, at the threshold of his great adventure, he went humbly to this historic place to make offerings to her ancient gods to seek their help. With his childhood friend Hephaestion, he knelt before the supposed graves of Achilles and his companion Patroclus and

The Alexander Mosaic, discovered in the ruins of Pompeii, was copied from a painting made 13 years after the Macedonian chased Darius from the field at Issus in 333 B.C. Made from tiny stone and glass tiles, the partly destroyed mosaic shows Alexander (left) in vigorous pursuit of the clearly terrified Darius.

Persian war chariots usually carried both a driver and an archer. In 333 B.C., however, for his last stand against Alexander, Darius created a new weapon: a four-horse, one-man battle car, armed with razor-sharp blades.

A symbolic map of Troy pinpoints the battle sites mentioned in the *Iliad*, Alexander's favorite book. He had been taught since childhood that he was descended from both Achilles and Paris, the opposing heroes of the Trojan War.

paid them tribute. Then he left his armor at the shrine of Athena, the patron goddess of Troy, and took in its place a shield said to have been used in the legendary war.

With this sacred trophy before him, Alexander marched boldly into the Persian Empire with his 35,000 men. He might still have been stopped by the vast armies of the East, but once again Darius failed to take the measure of his enemy. He arrogantly sent a small force of Greek mercenaries and Persian cavalry against him, and stayed comfortably and safely out of the action himself.

The general of the mercenaries, Memnon, was a Greek himself, and knew what he was up against. He suggested starving the invaders out by destroying the crops and burning the cities around him. He knew the Macedonians were skillful fighters but would be unable to survive for long without fresh supplies. Unfortunately for the Persians, the advice was contemptuously rejected by the Great King's commanders. The Persians were sure they could crush this little Macedonian force in open combat. At the Granicus River, they had their first chance to see how wrong they were.

The Persian army, for this battle at least, was probably smaller than Alexander's. It was arranged in simple formation along the eastern bank of the river, cavalry in front and infantry supporting them from behind. It was the usual Persian defensive formation, and it made things very difficult for the Macedonians, who had to cross a deep, rapid river

with steep banks to attack their enemy.

The Macedonian army reached the river a few hours before nightfall. Instead of waiting till the next day, Alexander immediately drew up his forces into battle formation on the bank opposite the Persians. With trumpets blaring, the heavy cavalry on the right wing plunged into the river. Alexander himself, his armor gleaming in the setting sun and with the two great white plumes of his helmet visible for a mile, led the charge.

Supported on the left by the slower moving infantry commanded by Parmenion, Alexander made straight for the mounted noblemen gathered in the center of the Persian forces. Alexander's horsemen had a difficult time scrambling up the slope at first, but they pushed ahead and drove deep into the Persian cavalry.

Alexander remained in the thick of the fight. His spear broken at the first thrust, he snatched up another and galloped straight for the Persian commander, Mithradates, who was Darius's son-in-law. But he was too late—the Persian noble hurled his light lance with deadly aim straight through the brightly polished Trojan shield and deep into Alexander's breastplate. Alexander snatched the javelin out and spurred Bucephalus on, driving his spear through Mithradates' armor and knocking him off

According to the *Iliad*, the Trojan War began when Paris, son of the king of Troy, kidnapped Helen, wife of the Greek king. After ten bloody years (1210–1200 B.C.), it ended when the Greeks duped the Trojans into admitting a huge wooden horse—secretly filled with Greek warriors—into their city.

Heinrich Schliemann (1822–1890), a wealthy German-American archeologist, searched the *Iliad* for clues to Troy's location. He discovered the site of the ancient city after extensive excavations during an 1872–74 expedition.

Alexander and Hephaestion visit the grave of Achilles in Troy. Following an ancient custom, the two friends and their companions then stripped and ran a ceremonial race around the tomb, which they later crowned with a wreath.

his horse. A contemporary report says that both armies cheered at this magnificent show of skill and courage.

Mithradates drew his short sword, still ready to fight from the ground, and as Alexander thrust his sword through him another Persian nobleman slashed at the Macedonian king, chopping through the plumed helmet and laying Alexander's head open to the bone. Alexander whirled around and struck his new assailant with such force he killed him instantly. But as he struck, the nobleman's brother came up from behind with sword upraised to finish him off. The Persian sabre was descending when Cleitus, another of Alexander's friends from school days, swung his sword and cut off the Persian assailant's arm at the shoulder with a single blow. Alexander, his head streaming blood, fell to the ground unconscious.

The battle continued to rage around him. At last Alexander regained consciousness and remounted Bucephalus. Rallying his cavalry, he struck yet again, deeper into the enemy center, and the Persian ranks broke. The Macedonians fought savagely and mercilessly. Memnon, seeing the cause was lost, retreated and petitioned for peace, but Alexander would give no quarter. His men butchered the enemy right and left, running them to the ground

and hacking them to pieces when they fell. Alexander's rage was especially directed at the Greek mercenaries, traitors to his cause of Greek unity. Thousands of them were slaughtered. Only 2,000 mercenaries survived the battle, and they were sent back in chains to work as slaves in the mines of Macedon. Alexander's own casualties were estimated at 150.

News of the victory spread fast through the Persian-governed Greek towns of Asia Minor's coast, and one by one they threw open their gates to "the Liberator." Sardis turned over its great treasury to him—money he badly needed by now—and Ephesus, Magnesia, and Tralles soon joined Sardis in welcoming him. In each, he set up a new, democratic government based on Greek law. Always his popularity was enhanced by the generous treatment he afforded those who surrendered. Even in Miletus, which resisted his march, he was lenient. The Greek mercenaries there so impressed him with their courage that he accepted them into his own army.

Besides Miletus, the only other place where Alexander encountered opposition was at Halicarnassus (present-day Bodrum, in Turkey), where his great antagonist Memnon commanded a powerful force. This was the strongest and best-fortified city Alexander had yet besieged, and he came close to losing his first engagement there. The Macedonian troops suffered heavy casualties, but at last Memnon was forced to evacuate. He burned the armory and equipment, salvaged what he could of the stores, and escaped with his remaining men. By the winter of 334 B.C., Alexander was securely placed in the major stronghold of the region.

Sending Parmenion with the cavalry to fight the tribes in the central plateau, Alexander gave a long-overdue furlough to all the newly married Macedonians in his army, naturally a very popular decision. He then moved east to secure the coast. His troops and Parmenion's were scheduled to meet again in the spring at Gordium in central Asia Minor. His march was slow, but steady progress was made. Nothing stood in his way. The slightest resistance was put down mercilessly. Most cities,

The exact location of Troy, which disappeared after the 4th century A.D., was unknown until archeologists began to find traces of the ancient city in the mid-19th century. This aerial photograph of its remains—the first ever published—appeared in 1936.

terrified by his reputation, submitted eagerly. Those that did not were crushed, and huge taxes were demanded of the "liberated" cities. When the governor of Aspendus objected to his demands for horses and tribute, Alexander doubled the demand and took the city's leading citizens as hostages. The objections were hastily withdrawn.

The spring of 333 B.C. saw Alexander at Gordium, his furloughed soldiers back refreshed, and his armies united. Gordium had a special tradition that Alexander found particularly fascinating. A wagon had been standing there for many years, with its yoke attached by a knot so tangled that no one could untie it. It was widely believed that the man who undid the Gordian knot would rule Asia. Of course, Alexander had to try.

Several versions of the story exist, but the one that has become legendary is that the king could not find a loose end and finally said, "What's the difference how I untie it?" Then he took his sword and cut through the knot with a single stroke.

Alexander's friend Cleitus moves in to defend his leader at the height of the Granicus River battle. When it was over, Alexander buried the dead Persian soldiers with the honors of war, thereby assuring them of peaceful passage to the afterworld. The gesture was regarded by both sides as unusually generous.

That is how Alexander was disposed to solving knotty problems. It is said that lightning and thunder followed the cutting of the Gordian knot—a sure sign to Alexander that the gods looked favorably upon his solution.

But if he was to be the Lord of Asia, he had one more problem to deal with—the job was already filled, and only the defeat of Darius III would leave it vacant.

Darius, then in his middle 40s, was a huge man, six and a half feet tall with a full black beard. He had become the Great King of Persia the same year that Alexander inherited the throne of Macedon. Darius was heir to a mighty empire and a vast army. But so far he had not proved himself a hero. The diminutive, fair-haired young Alexander, with his high voice and beardless face, already had an unbroken string of smashing victories behind him. He was determined to face the Lord of Asia down, like David before Goliath, and take his empire. Darius had haughtily held back from a personal confrontation till now, but he could not avoid the Macedonian forever.

At last, in October of 333 B.C., the two armies met. The first encounter was insignificant, but it established the spirit of the conflict. Darius attacked a hospital unit in the rear of the Macedonian encampment in the valley of Issus and butchered most of the injured soldiers recuperating there. The few he did spare had their hands severed. The unfortunate soldiers were then sent back to Alexander as symbols of Darius's might and ferocity. The Great King next ranged his men along the northern bank of the Pinarus River with Greek mercenary troops in front of him. He was protected in the rear by a strong fortification and the sea, and his army stood behind Alexander's, cutting off the Macedonians' line of communication with Parmenion.

It was a very unfavorable position for Alexander, and it left him no choice but to try a desperate frontal attack. Leading his personal regiment, the Companion Guard, Alexander charged into the massed ranks of archers on Darius's left. In mo-

You are each to observe the religions and customs, the laws and conventions, the feast days and festivities which you observed in the days of Darius. Let each stay Persian in his way of life, and let him live within his city....

For I wish to make the land one of widespread prosperity and employ the Persian roads as peaceful and quiet channels of commerce.
—ALEXANDER
in an edict to the citizens of conquered Persian towns

ments, his assault scattered the Persians, and the Macedonians turned their attention to the main body of troops in the center. Here Alexander could see the towering figure of Darius in his chariot amidst furious fighting. Alexander made straight for his foe, his sword flashing in the afternoon sun as he hacked his way toward the Persian king. As the historian Curtius describes the scene: "Then came the devastation of ruin. Around the chariot of Darius you would see lying the leaders of the highest rank . . . all prone upon their faces, just as they had fallen in the struggle. . . . Among them you would find famous governors and great generals; piled up around them a mass of foot soldiers and horsemen of meaner degree."

Darius, fearing for his life, jumped from his gilded royal chariot onto a smaller, lighter one. He seized the reins and turned it around, desperately lashing the horse as he made his escape.

His confidence shattered, Darius looks for an escape route from the pandemonium on the Issus battlefield. The Great King, once renowned for his bravery, lost his nerve when he saw Alexander and his cavalry thundering toward him; thousands of his own men were trampled to death after he fled the field.

Alexander and Hephaestion inspect Darius's royal tent after the Persian king's flight from Issus. Appointed like a palace, the tent contained gold and silver tableware, inlaid furniture, an elaborate bath, and a throne. The loot abandoned by Darius included 3,000 gold talents.

This turned the tide of battle. Until that point the two sides had been evenly matched, and the Persians had a good chance of winning. At the sight of their leader fleeing, however, they lost courage and frantically followed him, the Macedonian cavalry in hot pursuit.

Alexander raced after Darius. Arrian reports that he and his men rode across a ravine on the bodies of dead soldiers, such was the devastation of the battle. But Darius had too good a head start. The Great King, abandoning even his light chariot, had stripped off his royal cloak, dropped his shield and bow, and jumped on the bare back of a horse to ride to safety as night fell. The chariot and royal insignia were found, and Alexander took them back to camp as trophies.

Back at Issus, he found other, greater trophies waiting for him. The royal tent of Darius, abandoned in the Great King's flight, contained the rich personal effects of the king and appointments more luxurious than anything the Macedonian had ever seen. "So this," he is reported to have said as he sat down to the splendid feast that had been intended for Darius, "is what it is to be a king!"

6

Pharaoh

An incident that followed Alexander's defeat of Darius throws light upon an interesting aspect of his character. Darius had been so sure of himself and his army in the field that he had traveled with his entire household, and they were all still in the camp at Issus. As Alexander finished his victory banquet, he heard the crying of women. When he investigated, he learned that the Persian king had abandoned his mother, his wife, and his three children. When they saw Alexander carrying Darius's cloak back as a trophy, they naturally supposed that Darius was dead.

Alexander was always gallant in his treatment of women and strictly forbade his soldiers to violate those they captured. He made no exception of his enemy's family. Expecting the usual fate of captives, Darius's family prostrated themselves before him, but he raised them up tenderly, told them that Darius was still alive, and assured them that they would be treated as if they were at home. Instead of claiming the Persian queen—a famous beauty—for his prize, he had her and her family carefully protected and allowed them the continued enjoyment of all their former privileges and honors. He treated Darius's mother, Sisygambis, with such respect and consideration that she became

The four faces of the Egyptian god Ammon symbolize earth, water, fire, and air—the elements of which the ancients believed the universe was composed. Alexander, like all his countrymen, showed complete tolerance for foreign gods.

The inscrutable stare of a sphinx greeted Alexander when he entered Memphis, the ancient capital of Egypt, in 332 B.C. Its sightless eyes still fixed on the Nile, the Memphis sphinx is one of several such huge creations surviving from antiquity.

Alexander usually moved his army quickly, but he took his time crossing Mesopotamia, sticking to the cooler uplands and their palm-filled oases. During the march, his omen-conscious troops were alarmed by an eclipse of the moon; Alexander soothed them by explaining that the darkened moon symbolized Persia.

his fast friend. When he died, she was so heartbroken that, according to legend, she refused to eat for five days and at last turned her face to the wall and died.

Darius, now a fugitive, had no way of knowing of Alexander's generous treatment of his family, and sent him a message offering to ransom them. He agreed to pay whatever price Alexander demanded and to sign a truce giving the Macedonian possession of all the cities of Asia west of the Halys River. This had been Alexander's original goal—the taking of the Greek-populated area of western Asia. Certainly, it was all his father had ever set out to accomplish. By now, however, a taste for conquest had taken possession of Alexander, and he was not about to be paid off, as he said, with what he already had. His answer—maybe in part to goad Darius into open combat—reflected a mixture of pride, confidence, and deliberate insolence. The 23-year-old began his letter to the middle-aged Great King, "King Alexander to Darius," and he went on to make it clear that he now considered himself to be the Great King of Persia. He concluded with the insulting challenge: "If you wish to dispute your throne, stand up and fight for it, and do not run away. Wherever you hide, I will find you."

Darius had no choice but to begin organizing a new army, and this gave Alexander time to rest and plan his future. First there was the question of money, a constant problem for Alexander. He once said that he had inherited from his father a few gold cups and less than 60 talents, along with a debt of 500 talents, and that he had had to borrow 800 more to prepare for his war. The plunder gained along the way had just about met his expenses, but there were always troops to be paid and supplies to be bought. For all his triumphs, Alexander always seemed a few talents in arrears, and now that he had a respite from battle he was determined to rectify the situation.

Accordingly, he sent his general Parmenion to take Damascus, capital of present-day Syria and

Damascus in the early 20th century. At that time the city probably looked much as it did when it surrendered to Parmenion in 333 B.C. The vast treasure yielded by Damascus, which included the war chest of the Great King and the private riches of his nobles, relieved Alexander of his worries about paying for his Persian campaign.

A medieval drawing shows Alexander conferring with his officers before the siege of Tyre. The Tyrians' response to Alexander's peace overtures was demonstrated by their treatment of his emissaries: At right, two of them sink in the channel while a third is thrown from a parapet.

then the treasure-house of the Persian Empire. Parmenion had little trouble seizing the city and its treasury. With this accomplished, Alexander at last felt financially secure. The fact that he no longer needed Macedonian or Greek support may have contributed to his subsequent preoccupation with the idea of marching further eastward.

Alexander was anxious to capture or kill Darius and take his crown, but he was patient enough to secure his own position before rushing headlong after him. He knew the Persians were preparing to attack Greece, hoping thus to sever his lines of supply and communication. If he could occupy the Phoenician towns, which harbored the best ships and crews of the Persian fleet, he would control the entire eastern Mediterranean coast. And in fact, one by one, the towns of the coast did open their gates to welcome Alexander as a liberator.

Only Tyre held out. This great, independent Phoenician city was the principal commercial center of the Mediterranean world. It had withstood 13 years of constant siege from King Nebuchadnezzar of Babylon and was not about to surrender to Alexander without a fight. Tyrian society was highly advanced and boasted a technological base equal to any in the world at that time. Tyre was also a powerful island fortress, protected in part by a deep, mile-wide channel and enclosed on all sides by thick stone walls 150 feet high. A skilled and experienced fleet added to its security.

Alexander, as usual, sent envoys offering peace

And in future when you send to me, send to the lord of Asia; and do not write to me what to do, but ask me, as master of all you own, for anything you need. Or I shall judge you an offender. If you claim your kingdom, take your stand and fight for it, and do not run; for I shall make my way wherever you may be.
—ALEXANDER
in a letter to Darius, 333 B.C.

and urging the Tyrians to join him. Their quick response, in full view of the Macedonians, was to kill the ambassadors and throw their bodies off the towering stone walls into the sea. Alexander understood this answer all too well and immediately prepared to exact revenge.

At first glance a siege of Tyre looked impossible. The city was all but impregnable. Beyond artillery range, protected by its mountainous walls, and defended by a large, powerful navy, Tyre could seemingly withstand any assault.

Even the infuriated Alexander realized that taking Tyre would not be easy. Early in 332 B.C. he

Atop a portable, catapult-armed tower, Alexander supervises work on the 200-foot-wide causeway he constructed to gain access to Tyre. The Tyrians destroyed the tower with a fireship, but Alexander ordered it rebuilt.

By removing some of the rust from ancient Greek spears, modern archeologists have discovered that the spearheads were carefully forged to make them as resistant to breakage as possible.

called his council together and asked its advice. Should he abandon the proposed siege and simply continue his pursuit of Darius, or should he try to capture Tyre and then, if successful, continue down the coast to Egypt, and plunder it for the pleasures and riches that it reputedly had to offer? He made his own preference quite clear when he reminded his advisors that, since the Spartans were trying to stir up a rebellion at home, little support could be expected from the other Greek states. Only if they immediately secured their position here would they stand a chance of taking Asia, which now lay before them like a precious jewel. His argument carried the day, as usual, and his men again readied for military action.

Since he could not attack the city from the water, Alexander hit upon the idea of building a causeway—a road of stone and cedar beams—to span the mile that separated them from the city.

The Tyrians harassed the road builders fiercely, raining arrows on them from their boats. Captured Macedonians were always tortured to death. The Tyrians poured red hot sand down on the Macedonian workers, burning their flesh until, as the historian Diodorus described it, "they screamed entreaties like men under torture . . . went mad and died." The workers were sprayed with "Greek fire," a mixture of pitch, sulphur, and naphtha, which was inextinguishable even in the water. But still the road continued to grow until, after long, expensive months, it came close enough for Alexander, now assisted by ships from other Phoenician cities, to attack. Great battering rams were fixed to the decks of Alexander's ships, and catapults rained heavy stones from the road. Once the thick walls broke, the Macedonians poured in.

With all their sophistication and ferocity, the Tyrians were no match for Alexander and his men, and in August 332 B.C. the great Mediterranean port of Tyre crumbled before him. Over 8,000 Tyrians were killed, and 30,000 were captured and sold into slavery. But Alexander did not subject Tyre to the same treatment that he had meted out to Thebes. Instead of razing it to the ground, he

Tyrian soldiers retreat as Macedonian troops storm their island fortress through a breach made by a battering ram. At the same time, Alexander's ships attacked the Tyrian ships defending the harbor, and a column of infantry entered the city over the massive causeway.

resettled the city and established it, under Macedonian command, as his principal stronghold.

He now held the entire eastern Mediterranean coast. The Persian navy had been for the most part dispersed, and the Phoenician fleet was under his command. He had accomplished what Philip had set out to do.

While Alexander was besieging Tyre, he received a second and even more humble letter from Darius, offering 10,000 talents (estimated in the 1940s as about $18,000,000) as ransom for his family. Darius also proposed, as he had before, to negotiate a peace treaty and to cede to Alexander the entire western part of the Persian Empire. As an additional incentive, Darius offered the hand of one of his daughters in marriage.

These remarkable concessions stood to yield the young Macedonian even greater dominion than his

After rejecting the peace
offer that Darius sent him at
Tyre, Alexander turned his
attention to the conquest of
Egypt, an exotic land boast-
ing an ancient civilization
whose greatest monuments
were pyramids (royal tombs)
such as those pictured below.

father had originally sought. Nevertheless, Alexander considered them insufficient. Against the advice of his oldest and most trusted general, he
rejected Darius's overtures. As the German historian Ulrich Wilcken has written in his *Alexander
the Great:* "It was a fateful moment for the ancient
world. If Alexander had been satisfied . . . the whole
evolution of ancient civilization would have been
totally different. The aftereffects of his decision,
indeed, stretch through the Middle Ages down to
our own day, in the East as in the West. . . . There
never could have been that worldwide culture, whose
effects can be traced to India and even to China. . . .
We see here . . . what a decisive effect the will of
Alexander had on the subsequent history of the
world."

Some of his soldiers wanted to take the riches
and go home; the Greeks wanted him to stop drain-
ing their treasury for conquests that meant little to
them; and of course the Persians wanted him to
leave them alone—everyone agreed that he had done
enough. However, Alexander knew that if he stopped
now, the still-powerful Persian Empire would probably regroup its forces and attack him. He had no
wish to be put on the defensive, now that he had
Darius on the run. Alexander's urge to push on
was insatiable. Nothing and no one could stop him
now.

With Tyre secured, Alexander continued his march to the south, meeting opposition only at Gaza, where another siege resulted in another victory. Now nothing stood between Alexander and Egypt. In a week he reached Pelusium, the first fortress on the border of that already ancient kingdom.

Although Alexander was prepared to fight, it became unnecessary when Egypt promptly opened its doors to him and handed over its entire treasury of 800 talents. It did so not from fear but with joy and relief. The sacred country of the *pharaohs* (Egypt's kings) had been conquered and occupied by the Persians only 10 years before, and considered itself an oppressed nation. The Persians had exiled their king, sacked their temples, and imposed their religion on the people. Thus, Alexander came to them not as a conqueror but as a liberator.

It was typical of the Hellenic spirit to accept other religions. In fact, the Greeks often simply incorporated the gods and beliefs of other peoples into their own. Experts on Greek religion agree that they had done this for centuries. In any case, when the Macedonian king marched into Memphis (near Cairo, the present-day capital of Egypt), he restored all the holy places and declared the chief Egyptian god Ammon to be the same as the Greek Zeus.

The Egyptians considered their rulers to be gods, or at least the sons or reincarnations of gods, so when Alexander accepted the crown of the pharaoh in November 332 B.C., he accepted the divine status that accompanied his new role. There is a story that when he approached the oracle of Ammon—then called Zeus-Ammon—at Siwah, the Egyptian priest mispronounced the Greek words for "My son" and called him "God's son." Alexander did not object. His mother, after all, had always insisted that his father had been a god. Whether or not Alexander really believed it, he did on occasion, perhaps in jest, refer to himself in divine terms. And it was good political policy as well, since the Egyptians seemed to enjoy being ruled by a god.

As the incarnation of a god, Alexander held unlimited power in Egypt. Among the Macedonians he always had to submit his ideas to his generals

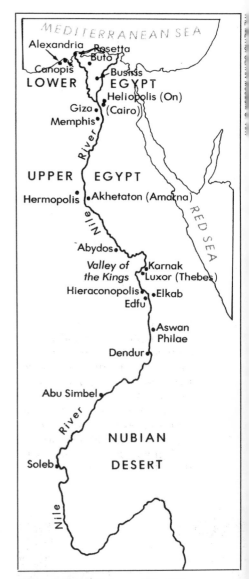

After marching up the Nile River to Memphis, Alexander returned to the Mediterranean coast, where he chose the location for the new city of Alexandria. His exploration of the site must have brought him—unknowingly, of course—to the exact place where his tomb would someday rise.

and counselors. It was not so, however, in Egypt. There, his every utterance was accepted as divine law.

Alexander soon began to organize Egypt as a province. To ensure the Egyptians' good will, he appointed two natives as civilian governors (with two Macedonian military governors in charge of the troops stationed there), and he left the collecting of taxes to the Egyptians. After 10 years of harsh Persian rule, the new province was profoundly grateful to be under Alexander's somewhat more benevolent sway.

As a former student of Aristotle, he had never lost sight of the values that his old tutor had instilled in him, and he encouraged scientific investigation whenever he could. At Aristotle's request, he sent a group of scholars to the Sudan to explore the reason for the annual flooding of the Nile—a question that had occupied the minds of Greek scientists for years. The expedition discovered that it was the heavy rains in mountains to the south that caused the Nile to overflow every summer. Thus the puzzle was solved for all time.

But Alexander's scientists performed a much more important service for him and for the world during his half-year stay in Egypt. They helped him select a site for a new city.

He had not founded a city since he began his long march from Macedon, but now he realized that he needed to establish an administrative capital. More importantly, he wanted a commercial center—a focus for trade between East and West. To create a worldwide empire it was not enough to conquer. It was necessary to build as well, and the economic future of his territory was as important to Alexander as any consideration of its military viability. He needed a good harbor for his warships, but a good port for shipping was just as vital. An ideal place would be a point on the Mediterranean near one of the mouths of the Nile.

With the advice of the scientists who always accompanied his army, Alexander chose a spot on a narrow ridge between Lake Mareotis and the sea, just across from the sacred Island of Pharaohs.

The ruins of an ancient Egyptian temple are partially submerged by the waters of the Nile, backed up after construction of the Aswan High Dam in 1970. Egypt's culture is 6,000 years old; by the time of Alexander's conquest in 332 B.C., it had been an independent nation for more than 30 centuries.

The small island helped create a deep harbor sheltered from the sea, and the lake a good inner harbor. They were both easy to defend, and the climate in the region was consistently temperate. Most important of all, however, the ridge was west of the westernmost mouth of the Nile. The sea current, flowing from west to east here, deposited tons of silt from the river every year, and every other harbor on the Egyptian coast had been silted up over the years. Only here was the harbor free from this deposit.

Never given to modesty, he named the city Alexandria. It was one of the estimated 70 towns that bore his name, and the only one that has survived and grown. Now, more than 2,000 years after its foundation, it is the second city and principal port of Egypt.

With the help of Deinocrates, a specialist in urban planning who had designed Ephesus when that city was rebuilt, he laid Alexandria out on a grid system. Like modern New York, it was designed with broad, major streets running in one direction and closer, narrower ones crossing them at right angles. Houses, shops, temples, and government buildings were erected on the square blocks formed by this pattern. It was, and remains, a thoroughly modern city.

Alexandria almost immediately replaced the ravaged Tyre as the major commercial and trade center in the region. In time it became the first truly international city. Persians and Greeks, Macedonians and Jews, Indians and Africans were all drawn by the opportunities available in this busy port. As they worked together in Alexandria, the fusion of Greek and Oriental culture that came to be known as Hellenism began to develop and spread, and the cultures of both East and West were changed. "There can be no doubt," wrote Alexander Robinson in his *Alexander the Great* "that this was the most important concrete result of Alexander's life."

It was important to him, too, but perhaps not the most important thing at that moment. He still had a king to capture and an empire to conquer.

Alexander built the harbor of Alexandria around Pharos Island, where a huge lighthouse was built c. 200 B.C. Destroyed by an earthquake in 1375, the 400-foot-tall Pharos lighthouse was one of antiquity's fabled Seven Wonders of the World.

7

Hunter

Alexander was a hunter. He had loved the hunt since early childhood, and in every new country he entered he indulged this fancy, tracking and shooting whatever he could. Competitive sports never excited him so much as the thrill of the chase. Now he was after the biggest game of his life—the Great King of Persia.

Darius knew he was being stalked. He scoured what was left of his empire to rebuild his army. The western part was already in Alexander's hands, so the Great King recruited the fierce Bactrian and Sogdian tribesmen from eastern Iran. He rounded up soldiers from every village and collected elephants from India, beyond his empire. Most modern historians estimate the total of his infantry at 200,000, his cavalry at 40,000.

But he knew now that massive numbers were not enough. He would also have to change his tactics if he wanted to avoid repeating the experiences of the battles of Granicus and Issus.

The first thing he did was arm his cavalry with spears, since the javelins they had used formerly had been ineffective against the Macedonian lances. Then, remembering the deadly use Alexander made of phalanxes, Darius constructed special chariots with scythes on their wheels and long spears attached to a pole in front, hoping to mow down the tightly massed Macedonians like wheat. Finally, because he felt that his men had been hindered by

I will not steal my victory.
—ALEXANDER
refusing Parmenion's request that he
make a surprise attack, 331 B.C.

The Euphrates River makes its leisurely way across Asia Minor just as it did in Alexander's time. To enable the Macedonian to move on to his last great battle with Darius, his advance engineers threw a temporary bridge across the wide but slow-moving river.

Silver coins made by Alexander's mints became the universal currency of the ancient world. A heroic image of the Macedonian king often embellished the coins; this one, copied from a sculpture in a shrine at Sparta, shows Alexander as the mythical hero Heracles.

A pebble mosaic shows the rescue of Alexander (left) by Craterus (d. 321 B.C.), one of the Macedonian's most important generals as well as his close friend. Like all his countrymen, Alexander loved to hunt; during his Asian campaigns, he often stalked lions between battles.

When the Macedonian horses, with Alexander himself at the head of them, vigorously pressed the assault, fighting hand to hand and thrusting at the Persians' faces with their spears, and the infantry phalanx in close order and bristling with pikes added its irresistible weight, Darius, who had been on edge since the battle began and now saw nothing but terror all round him, was the first to turn tail and ride for safety.

—ARRIAN
writing on the Battle of Gaugamela

the cramped space of Issus, he chose a large plain for what he expected to be the battleground. He leveled it even further to extend the area in which his scythe-bearing carts could operate. Then he waited.

Alexander knew exactly where Darius was. In July 331 B.C. he decided it was time to move. So he marched north to the Euphrates River and then east toward Mesopotamia—present-day Iraq—to meet the Lord of Asia at last.

The two played a desperate game of tag for a while. Darius tried to draw the Macedonians to his prepared plain, northwest of Babylon, where he had his great force waiting, but Alexander recognized the trap in time and made a quick detour. Darius changed his plans accordingly and found a second, almost equally favorable battleground. Once more, Alexander altered his route, forcing Darius to change his plans yet again. Finally, the Persian set up his camp at Gaugamela (now Tell Gomel), cleared the ground for his chariots and prepared for what he knew would be a tough fight.

Darius's recognition of Alexander's military genius can be seen from the fact that, rather than offering battle immediately, he sent the Macedonian king a third letter, whose terms were even more generous than those contained in his previous pieces of panic-stricken correspondence. Again, he tendered the entire western territory of his empire—which Alexander laughed at because he already held it—and one of his daughters in marriage. Then he increased the ransom for the rest of his family to 30,000 talents—about $54,000,000—and, for good measure, offered his son Ochus as a permanent hostage. Again Alexander's generals recommended that he accept. And again Alexander said no. The issue was to be decided by bloodshed rather than bribes.

The Macedonian infantry numbered some 40,000 and the cavalry a scant 7,000, so Darius's troops outnumbered them by about 5 to 1. Perhaps Alexander did not realize that when he threw the Great King's last bid for peace back in his face, but he came to learn it soon afterward.

On September 30, Alexander climbed a hill above Gaugamela and beheld the forces Darius had mustered. It was a staggering sight. The Persian cavalry seemed to stretch to the horizon, and the great, bristling scythed chariots—said to number 200—were like modern tanks. To anyone but Alexander such an army might have seemed invincible.

Parmenion suggested a surprise assault at night, but Alexander knew the Persians were fully armed and waiting. Besides, he said, he wanted to earn his victory honestly. He told his men to eat heartily and get a good night's sleep, so as to be fresh for battle the next morning. That would reduce some of the advantage held by the enemy, who would spend the night nervously waiting for a possible Greek attack. Then he went into his own tent to make his battle plan.

On the dawn of October 1, 331 B.C., Alexander was the last one up. He had slept so deeply that it was necessary to shake him awake. His confidence was encouraging to his men. "What do I have to worry about," he is said to have asked his nervous generals, "when Darius is finally ready to fight? He has done exactly what I wanted!"

Parmenion was not so sure of success. With 34,000 cavalry to Alexander's 7,000, the Persians extended nearly a mile beyond the Macedonian line.

Although this 18th-century tapestry was called "The Battle of Arbela," the actual events at Arbela, the Persian base camp, were considerably calmer. When Alexander pursued Darius there after the Battle of Gaugamela, he found the camp almost deserted and discovered that the Great King had fled.

But Alexander had devised a daring and inventive tactic, one that has been copied by generals in similar circumstances ever since. Knowing that he was outnumbered, he planned to give the enemy an idea that his forces were even weaker than they were. He would use his left and right flanks to draw as many of the Persians as he could onto the sides. Then, when the enemy center showed an opening, he would drive his phalanx into it.

The battle started cautiously, both sides avoiding a head-on confrontation. The Persian right flank was quickly pulled away into an engagement with the Macedonian left. The Persian left wing was commanded by Bessus, the governor of Bactria and a formidable fighter. At Darius's command, he thrust against Alexander's right flank. Parmenion was holding the Persian right, and Alexander kept feeding reserves to keep Bessus busy on the Persian left. At this point, Darius unleashed the scythed chariots, determined to shatter the phalanx before it could strike.

Alexander had had some experience with this tactic and was ready for it. Just as the Thracians had failed to crush his men with their carts some years earlier, so the scythed carts of the Persians proved no more effective. Alexander had placed quick, agile troops in front of his phalanx, and these keen marksmen jabbed at the horses, pulling down the drivers and stabbing them. The chariots went out of control and many turned over. The few that reached the massed troops were useless—the phalanx simply opened its ranks and let them pass. As one historian has observed, scythed chariots are useful only if the enemy stands still.

Alexander kept his main striking force ready and continued to send in reinforcements to occupy the Persians' right and left flanks. More and more of Darius's center force was drawn into the struggle, and at last a hole appeared in the line. Lashing Bucephalus into action, Alexander galloped into battle at the head of his Companion Guard, which had been deployed in wedge formation. Alexander drove deep into the Persian gap and then wheeled his horsemen to the left, toward Darius. Mean-

Astride Bucephalus, Alexander thunders into the center of the Persian line at Gaugamela. This was the last battle for the 24-year-old warhorse; Alexander took affectionate care of the gallant old animal until its death five years later, but he never again exposed Bucephalus to war.

while, the phalanx crashed into the front of Darius's center line.

Bessus was barely holding his own on the left and was powerless to help. Recognizing that his situation was deteriorating, he ordered his Bactrian troops to retreat to safety. The Persian right was also in confusion and had lost contact with the center. Darius saw that he was facing the full force of the Macedonian phalanx and that he had no support from either side. It was the Battle of Issus all over again. In a panic, he whirled his chariot around and fled.

Seeing the Great King galloping away, the disheartened commander of the Persian right wing took off after him and left the field to Parmenion. Bessus, on the Persian left, was already gone. Once again, Darius's army had fallen victim to Alexander's superior generalship.

Alexander was now so close to his quarry that he could almost sense Darius's presence. He spurred Bucephalus on after the Great King until nightfall, and then resumed the pursuit after midnight. But Darius had too great a head start and again avoided capture. Alexander found his chariot and bow—he was beginning to build up a collection of Darius's military equipment—this time something extra was added to his battle souvenirs. In his flight the Persian king had left behind his personal fortune, and the Macedonians came upon 4,000 talents—over $7,000,000—in gold coins. It had been a good day's work.

Eager as he was to follow the scent and run Darius to the ground, Alexander decided to see what he had won from him first. Darius could wait. His power was effectively shattered, along with his army and personal prestige. The Macedonians could afford to take their time and enjoy some of the rewards of their efforts. Three great, rich cities, the principal centers of the Persian Empire, lay waiting to be entered.

The first was Babylon, an important city in the ancient kingdom of Assyria and capital of Nebuchadnezzar's Babylonian Empire. Its outer walls were 180 feet thick and 400 feet high, and they sur-

As king of Babylon, Alexander shrewdly reconfirmed the governorship of Mazaeus, who had been defeated at Gaugamela by Parmenion. As well as pleasing the Persians, this appointment was welcomed by the Macedonians, since paying tribute to the courage of an opponent was considered a compliment to the victor.

Standing on the remains of a brick pavement, an archeologist inspects part of the ruins of Babylon, once the most important city in western Asia. The metropolis, which had received Alexander in glory in 331 B.C., was the scene of his death eight years later.

rounded 60 square miles of land. As Alexander rode up to its gate, ready for another siege, he was met by its governor—the general who had fought Parmenion at Gaugamela—coming out with his children to surrender.

Babylon, "the soul of the East," had been a mighty, independent city that at one time had claimed "world sovereignty." But Xerxes, the son of Darius I, had destroyed its main temple and taken away its independence 123 years before Alexander was born. Now, like the Egyptians, the people of Babylon welcomed Alexander as their savior. They burned incense and threw flowers before his chariot as he entered. They also gladly turned their treasury over to him. As he had done in Egypt, he restored their ancient temple and their sovereignty, reappointed the native governor, and welcomed them into his empire as an independent province. To his many other titles could now be added king of Babylon.

The Macedonians spent a luxurious month in this beautiful old city as the welcome guests of its grateful people, enjoying its wine, its women, and the famous terraces of trees and shrubs known as the Hanging Gardens. Alexander was no less generous to his men than the Babylonians. He lavished gifts and bonuses on his soldiers, issuing them almost an extra year's pay. It must have been tempting to stay on. But new delights awaited them.

The second great city of Darius's empire was Susa, his administrative capital, about 400 miles to the east of Babylon. Here was an even choicer piece of booty, whose 50,000 talents—some $90,000,000—were a welcome contribution to the Macedonians' funds after Alexander's extravagant generosity at Babylon. This was Xerxes' great hoard, much of it looted from Greece over a century before. Again Alexander doled out gifts with reckless abandon.

One more city remained to enter—the most important of all, Persepolis, "City of Persia" and capital of the empire. Like Mecca or Jerusalem or Rome, Persepolis was a holy city and it housed the Persian royal palace and treasury. This city was not as easy to take as Babylon or Susa. To enter it Alexander

had to go through the narrow mountain pass known as the Persian Gates. There he encountered stiff opposition from the last holdouts of Darius's army. Eventually he was able to break through to the holy city before the garrison there could loot it and flee.

In Persepolis Alexander found the greatest treasure of his entire expedition: more than 120,000 talents—about a half a billion dollars. This was more than the entire national income of Athens in its 300-year golden age.

The Persian emperors had always stored their gold and silver as bullion, coining it as needed and depending on their reserves for emergencies. But Alexander had different ideas. He was primarily interested in unifying the various parts of the empire he was creating. To encourage commerce and make trading easier he set about at once to centralize the financial administration of the lands he ruled. He also standardized the money of Greece and the Persian Empire. He minted the gold and silver he found and initiated great public works to

Alexander, drawn in a chariot plated with gold, receives a triumphal welcome to Babylon in 331 B.C. The walled Persian city was so large, wrote Aristotle, that it took two days for word of its surrender to reach all its people.

put it into circulation.

Once again Alexander appointed a native as governor of the province. This time, however, he took for himself the title of Great King. He had been calling himself that since the Battle of Granicus, but now he was actually sleeping in the Great King's bedchamber and sitting on his high golden throne.

Still, while Darius lived—and his holy city stood —it was only with his own troops that Alexander could claim this title. He knew that the Persians would never truly accept him. They might welcome his lavish gifts and remain obedient and fearful subjects, but in their eyes he was sure to remain more of a conqueror than their legitimate monarch. So Alexander, reasoning that if he could not graft himself onto the royal family tree and become the lawful heir to the throne, he might as well cut it down and plant his own. He instructed his soldiers to sack the city, an order they thoroughly enjoyed carrying out. He had restrained them in Babylon and Susa, but here finally was a chance for them to indulge their passion for destruction, and with royal approval at that! When the city had been looted to his men's satisfaction, Alexander

Babylon's Hanging Gardens were, like the great Pharos lighthouse at Alexandria, considered one of the ancient world's Seven Wonders. A series of terraces planted with elaborate ornamental greenery, the gardens were nourished by a complex irrigation system that drew water from the nearby Euphrates River.

issued a final order: to torch Xerxes' palace, the spiritual heart of Persepolis which for centuries had symbolized rule by the family of Darius. Today it would be tantamount to destroying the Vatican, an atrocity guaranteed to provoke condemnation. It made his point more emphatically than anything he had yet done. The dynasty of Cyrus, Xerxes, and Darius had indeed ended. Alexander of Macedon had taken their place in Persia.

Some later writers, seeking to justify, or at least explain, Alexander's harsh order, attributed it to an uncharacteristic fit of drunkenness. But modern historians reject this excuse as a lame attempt to downplay the fact that Alexander was perfectly capable of acting barbarically when it suited him. Few experts doubt that the burning of Xerxes' magnificent palace was a calculated move to destroy the symbol of the royal house of Darius. With it, Alexander brought his official mission of revenge to an end.

As early as the struggle in Tyre, word had reached Alexander that some of the Greek states were growing increasingly rebellious. An uprising in Crete threatened to grow into a full-scale revolution against his authority, Sparta was, as usual, provoking unrest, and Thrace was trying yet again to assert its independence. Alexander had sent a small fleet to support Antipater, his regent in Macedon. Now, in 330 B.C., Alexander learned that Antipater had successfully crushed the Spartan rebellion. While the affairs of Greece might have seemed trivial to Alexander at this point, the event was significant. It meant that the Hellenic peninsula was once again unified under his official command.

Alexander could now devote all his attention to one of his growing obsessions—hunting down the ever-elusive Darius.

The Great King had fled to the last of the Persian capitals, Ecbatana (now Hamadan), with the pitiful remnants of his army. Everything was in disarray for the once powerful leader and he was virtually reduced to running for his life. Ecbatana was the capital of Media and one of the few provinces still loyal to him. But it was a poor, barren place in

Burning the magnificent palace at Persepolis would, said Parmenion, make Alexander look more like a conqueror than a king, but Alexander ignored the advice of his argumentative general. Ironically, the destruction of the palace, and its subsequent long disappearance beneath the desert sands, resulted in its becoming the era's best preserved monument.

Bessus (left; d. 329 B.C.)—who would later learn the fearful consequences of betrayal—prepares to stab Darius with his javelin. Informed by one of Darius's supporters that the Great King was in mortal danger, Alexander made a breakneck dash to rescue his old enemy, but he was too late.

which he was not at all comfortable. He also knew that in a short time Alexander would be upon him. So, with 9,000 men and the small treasury of Ecbatana he wearily headed north, hoping against hope that he could cross the Kurdish mountains to eastern Iran before the possessed Macedonian overtook him.

Alexander got to Ecbatana a few days too late. Frustrating though it was, he at least had his prey within easy stalking distance. At this point Alexander decided to postpone the chase for a while to deal with some political problems at home.

Like his father, Alexander was at his best on the battlefield. As a general he was brilliant, and his men followed him with the loyalty and devotion that soldiers accord to none but the greatest commanders. Now, however, his Macedonian troops were becoming disturbed by the influence that Eastern habits were having on their leader. Some of his soldiers were muttering that success had gone to his head and that he had forgotten his original plans and promises. They were becoming increasingly annoyed at the favor he was showing the Persians, treating his new subjects as equals and even giving them positions in high office. Alexander had to call a general assembly of his Greek and Macedonian soldiers to win a vote of confidence. Though his persuasive manner and personal charm succeeded, as always, his popularity with his old troops was declining.

Alexander was too close to his goal now to devote much time to his discontented army. He left Parmenion—whose constant argumentativeness he had begun to find irritating—to take charge in Ecbatana and set out with 500 men after Darius.

Near Hecatompylos—about 250 miles from present-day Teheran—he discovered that Darius had escaped him for good.

As the Persian king had approached this little village with his small company, Bessus and another noble, Nabarzanes, told the Great King that his star had set and that he should step down from office. When he indignantly refused, they and a small group of conspirators seized him, put him in chains, and threw him in a wagon as a hostage to offer Alexander as a last resort. When Alexander's men drew near, Bessus and his followers panicked and stabbed Darius. Then they and the rest of the conspirators scattered. Soon after, the Macedonians finally found the Great King, but he was dying. And by the time Alexander got to his wagon, Darius was dead. So the quarry eluded the hunter at last.

Alexander threw his own cloak over the Great King's body and sent it back to Sisygambis in Persepolis for a royal funeral. The hunt was over, and there was no reason to indulge in further vindictiveness.

Nabarzanes, who had not fled with the others and who claimed to have had no part in Darius's murder, surrendered to Alexander. The Macedonian ruler, recognizing the propaganda value of such a gesture, immediately pardoned him. But Bessus returned to his native Bactria, now Afghanistan, and declared himself the new Great King of Persia under the name of Artaxerxes IV.

Alexander's full claim to the title was now frustrated by a pretender to the throne. A new hunt was on.

Alexander's men silently observe their leader's somber farewell to Darius, the man he had hunted for so long, and who was now beyond his reach. Just before he died, Darius praised Alexander's courage and said he wished the Macedonian good luck as the new Great King of Persia.

8

Tyrant

To Alexander, it was important that the ruling monarch surrender the throne formally. Only in that way could he lay claim to being the Great King in the eyes of the Persian Empire. If he had captured Darius, he might have claimed the title by right of conquest. Now he still had to fight for it, and he knew Bessus was popular enough to organize resistance. A long, hard campaign seemed inevitable.

Adding to his problem was the attitude of his men. They had shared in his war of revenge, they had gone along with his conquest of the empire, they had agreed to his desperate hunt for Darius. Now they thought the war was over. They wanted to go home.

But Alexander called his troops together and made a rousing speech; "We stand," he told them, "on the very threshold of victory." All that was left to do was to defeat Bessus—who, he assured them, was little more than a barbarian chieftain—and Persia would be theirs. Again they consented, but weariness and dissatisfaction were growing.

Alexander knew that this campaign would not prove to be as easy as he had indicated. Bessus was no half-savage Thracian, but a bold, skillful warrior, and his Bactrian and Sogdian troops would be fighting on familiar terrain. In fact, the Macedonians lost many men in the hills of Bactria be-

> *It was not his design to ransack Asia, like a robber, nor to despoil and ruin it...as afterward Hannibal pillaged Italy...but to subdue all under one form of government and to make one nation of mankind.*
> —PLUTARCH

Alexander is often pictured in ancient Eastern art as a mounted Persian warrior. During the search for Bessus, the royal horses—the faithful old Bucephalus among them—were stolen by local bandits. After Alexander threatened to devastate the entire region, Bucephalus was returned; relieved and grateful, Alexander rewarded the thieves.

An eagle-headed deity, one of the thousands worshiped by the Persians. Although Alexander remained faithful to the Greek gods he had been brought up to revere, he treated other religions with respect; his easy acceptance of "barbarian" ways engendered resentment among his fiercely nationalistic Macedonian troops.

Alexander informs his troops that, despite the death of Darius, the war will continue. He told his men that he would pay their expenses home if they chose to leave, but few accepted the offer. Alexander gave lavish gifts to those who elected to stay.

fore they saw the end of the pretender to the title of Great King.

Even the capture of Bessus, however, did not fulfill Alexander's dream. The Macedonians caught up with him at last in Sogdiana, now in Soviet Turkestan. When they saw their cause was lost, Bessus's men hastily turned him over to Alexander, who stripped him naked and tied him to a post with a wooden slave-collar around his neck. He then had him publicly whipped, cut off his nose and ears, and sent him back to Ecbatana charged with both regicide—the killing of the king—and rebellion against the new Great King, Alexander. The Medes and Persians at Ecbatana did not want to offend their new ruler. They tried Bessus in due Persian form, found him guilty as charged, and had him torn to pieces as punishment.

The downfall of Bessus did little to discourage others from attempting to succeed where he had failed. Bessus had drawn Sogdian soldiers into his service by allying himself with two powerful barons of the region, Spitamenes and Oxyartes. It was Spitamenes who left Bessus unprotected for Alexander to capture. Now the Sogdian chieftain, free of Bessus's authority, took up the challenge himself. He rallied his men to revolt and ordered the slaughter of the Macedonian garrisons at Alexander's outposts. Then he laid siege to Macedonian-held Maracanda (now Samarkand). In the spring of 328 B.C. Alexander set out on yet another hunt.

Spitamenes—the most dangerous and determined opponent Alexander had faced since Memnon—was a cunning adversary, a tough guerrilla fighter who led his fierce Sogdian horsemen on myriad lightning-swift raids that demoralized the Macedonians whose entire strategy was based on the set-piece battle. Moreover, he and his followers considered themselves to be fighting for their very independence. Spitamenes kept the Macedonian forces busy until near the end of 328 B.C.

Alexander's men were reaching the end of their endurance. Having grown increasingly frustrated with his failure to capture Spitamenes, Alexander realized that a final, decisive encounter was now necessary. He mobilized a vast force and planned an all-out attack. The very plan was enough. When Spitamenes' troops heard the news, they gave in, and "the great hero of Iranian independence" met the same fate as Darius and Bessus. Spitamenes' army surrendered and, as a token of good faith, made Alexander a gift of the Sogdian chieftain's head.

That broke the back of the resistance movement. Only some mopping-up operations remained. Oxyartes, the Bactrian ally of Spitamenes in the betrayal of Bessus, was firmly entrenched in a mountain fortress. This stronghold, known as the Sogdian Rock, in present-day Tadzhikistan, was considered impregnable. But despite the bitter cold, despite the growing resentment of his depleted troops, Alexander went on with the chase. In January 327

Guerrillas, some of them wearing captured Macedonian armor, prepare to swoop down on Alexander's army in Sogdiana, a region that is now part of Soviet Turkestan. The campaign that he fought in Sogdiana and neighboring Bactria was a hard one for Alexander; his adversaries not only refused to fight in traditional Greek style, they ignored the chivalric code of honor observed by Greek warriors.

A Persian miniature painting from the 15th century shows a scimitar-wielding Alexander, armed with a bow and arrows and wearing a pointed Persian helmet. The Macedonian leader became the supreme hero of Persian myth, which credited him with fabulous exploits in every arena from battlefield to bedroom.

B.C. he led what was left of his army to the siege. More than 2,000 of his men froze to death on the way.

Oxyartes and his troops laughed when Alexander called on them to surrender. The fortress was perched halfway up a sheer rock face, and the chieftain said Alexander would need soldiers who could fly to get at him there. This was just the sort of challenge Alexander could not resist. At once he called on his troops for mountain climbers, offering 12 talents—over $20,000—to the first to reach the top, 11 to the next, and so on. Macedon is a mountainous country, and climbing steep rocks was nothing new to its people. Having promised such prizes for success, Alexander had little trouble finding 300 men who were prepared to risk a secret night assault on the Sogdian Rock. About 30 fell to their deaths during the ascent, but by morning the rest, using ropes and iron tent pegs, were able to signal their king from the peak, high above the fortress. Again Alexander had tried the impossible and succeeded. He sent word to Oxyartes that if the chieftain wanted to see Alexander's flying soldiers, he could look up to the peak of his own mountain. The Sogdians and Bactrians were amazed and terrified. Although they outnumbered the small Macedonian group above them, they threw down their arms and surrendered at once.

The conquest of the Sogdian Rock was a great stroke, an accomplishment that added further to the growing legend of Alexander's invincibility. There also emerged from this victory an additional advantage, one that Alexander could not have foreseen. Oxyartes' daughter, Roxane, was one of the prizes. Alexander might have claimed her as part of the spoils of war, but apparently he fell in love with her—the first such experience for the chaste and ambitious young king.

Arrian reports that it was true love that made him choose to marry her in a traditional Bactrian ceremony rather than simply taking her captive, but the political advantages of the gesture could not have been lost on him. A powerful Bactrian father-in-law could do much to reconcile the rebel-

lious Iranian tribesmen to the fact of foreign invasion.

Alexander's marriage to Roxane did improve his relations with the Iranian tribes. His Macedonian troops, however, who had faced so much danger and suffering with him over the years, disapproved of his marriage to a barbarian. They were beginning to feel that he was turning Oriental himself and thus coming to have increasingly little in common with his comrades-in-arms. He was increasingly treating his defeated enemies as the equals of his own people. He had put Persians in charge of conquered cities, taken them into his army, and even placed them among his officers. That Alexander now seemed to have no qualms about introducing Persian customs into his own court did not sit well with his longest-serving followers.

Alexander and Roxane preside over their nuptial feast at the royal palace in Susa. Many of Alexander's followers were scandalized by the thought that Greek lands might someday be ruled by a child of "barbarian" heritage, but Alexander, as usual, did exactly as he wished.

A 14th-century illustration shows Alexander wearing the fluted hat and long robe of a Persian noble. Although his fellow Macedonians were disgusted by his adoption of "barbaric" dress, Alexander enjoyed wearing Persian clothes, particularly the shoes, which were designed to make their wearer look tall.

Alexander had started wearing Persian clothes, for instance—not as an eccentric personal taste but to show the Persians that he regarded them as his equals. He had conquered their bodies with his army, some said, and now he was trying to win their souls by adopting their dress.

The tough and hardy Hellenes thought this undignified, and considered Alexander's newfound preference for Persian luxuries distinctly unbecoming to a Macedonian warrior. As the tension between the king and his troops grew, Alexander became increasingly isolated from his soldiers. His situation reflected the fact that loneliness can be one of the prices of absolute power. Alexander began to distrust his oldest friends. He suspected disloyalty everywhere. And sometimes his suspicions were well founded.

In 330 B.C. he became the target of an assassination plot. Surprisingly, however, the conspiracy was not a reaction to his wider policies. A dissatisfied soldier, resentful of the harsh disciplinary measures to which he had been subjected, convinced some of his comrades to make an attempt on Alexander's life. The plot was thwarted with no great difficulty, but the king used it as an excuse to kill the son of his old general Parmenion. This arrogant young officer, commander of the Macedonian cavalry, had openly expressed disapproval of Alexander's behavior, and the king was savage in his retribution. The army could have accepted this harsh decision—they did not like the officer much anyway—but Alexander went further. He was sure that Parmenion, now in his seventies and immensely popular with the troops, could no longer be trusted, and he had the old man put to death too, just in case. For this, the Macedonian and Greek troops never forgave Alexander.

Perhaps the most shocking evidence of the transformations in Alexander's character came two years later, in 328 B.C. Cleitus, a childhood friend who had saved his life at the Granicus River battle, dared to criticize him at a party. The once-abstemious king had begun to drink heavily by then, and, on this occasion, he was thoroughly inebriated. He lost all control, seized a spear, and thrust it through his friend's heart.

Remorse kept him in bed for three days, but it did not improve his habits. As he became more estranged from his own people, his preference for Oriental company and customs increased. In 328 B.C., feeling he could no longer depend on Greek and Macedonian forces to keep order in his conquered lands, he determined to take his policy of racial fusion one step further. He drafted 30,000 Persian boys to learn Greek and receive Macedonian military training. To make matters worse in the eyes of the Greeks, he called these young men his "Successors," saying that they would be the backbone of his empire. He obviously saw them as the next generation of his army and was preparing them to take over from his own people.

Somewhat improbably, however, the first major confrontation between Alexander and his men involved the issue of court etiquette. The Persians normally prostrated themselves before their kings, and they continued the practice with Alexander. For the Persians it was simply a gesture of respect. But to the Greeks, prostration was appropriate only before a god, and they considered making such a gesture to a mortal both ridiculous and degrading. As far as the Greeks were concerned, bowing be-

Aristotle was appalled by reports that his former pupil, Alexander, had adopted the dress and etiquette of the Persians, and that he was conferring honors on these "barbarians." The philosopher corresponded regularly with Callisthenes, Alexander's court historian, and may have put him up to the criticism of Alexander that cost the young chronicler his life in 328 B.C.

Court philosophers try to comfort Alexander, racked with grief after drunkenly killing his friend and benefactor Cleitus, in 328 B.C.. He was finally consoled by a priest of the cult of Dionysus, who told Alexander he had been a victim of divine madness, and had done the deed when he was, literally, not himself.

fore a man was the mark of a slave. When Cassander, the son of Alexander's regent, Antipater had first seen a Persian prostrating himself in front of the king, he had laughed out loud. Alexander's official court historian, Callisthenes, a nephew of Aristotle and an important man in academic circles in Athens, said it was positively sacrilegious. Alexander was putting on airs and beginning, in all seriousness, to think of himself as a god.

The act of prostration seems a minor thing, but it was very important to Alexander. He felt that he had to emanate the kind of regal aura that the Persians expected from their rulers or risk losing a portion of their respect. He was so angry at Cassander's laughter that he snatched him by the hair and banged his head against the wall. As for Callisthenes, he found himself charged with conspiracy and was duly executed.

Some Greeks thought Alexander was becoming insane. His reputation was certainly suffering badly.

Alexander's last monumental journey took him through the Khyber Pass, the chief break in the towering mountain range that divides what are now Afghanistan and Pakistan. Negotiating the rugged, 33-mile-long pass, which is 6,825 feet above sea level, involved numerous battles with fierce local tribes.

The Macedonians believed that they had already encountered every danger. When they knew that a fresh war with the most warlike nations of India still remained, they were struck with fear and began to upbraid the king with mutinous mutterings.
—RUFUS QUINTUS CURTIUS
first-century Roman historian, in his
History of Alexander, on Alexander's
troops' reluctance to fight
during the Indian campaign

Even his old teacher, Aristotle, spoke out against him openly. The Greeks began to see Alexander as a typical Oriental despot, every bit as cruel and bloodthirsty as the barbarian Darius.

Alexander, however, was not about to let criticism interfere with his dreams. He had not come halfway around the world to argue with his men about matters of protocol. There were still lands to conquer and new things to see. The remaining Persian provinces to the east, in present-day India, drew him onward. In 327 B.C. he gathered his armies and set off eastward on yet another great expedition. It was to be his last.

9

Searcher

The Greeks did not really understand the geography of India. They thought it was a small peninsula bordered by the end of the earth, the endless "world-stream" called Ocean. If they could reach this easternmost boundary, Alexander's dream of a world state would be achieved.

He would not have to do it alone, either. He already had one ally in the former Persian province of Taxila. The rajah of that region, Taxiles (called Ambhi or Omphis in some sources), had offered to cede his large and rich capital to Alexander in return for support against a neighboring rajah. Nothing could have suited Alexander better. Disunity among his enemies was always to his advantage. After much fighting en route, Alexander's armies crossed the Indus River and entered Taxiles' territory in the spring of 326 B.C. At Taxila (now Takshacila, in the Punjab), Alexander accepted the rajah's surrender and prepared for the next stage of the campaign. He enlisted 5,000 Indian troops and began to scout the area.

The Macedonian army spent about four months in Taxila, and came to know something of the Indian way of life and thought. It was something altogether new to them, the first real meeting of

Taxiles, here attended by courtiers, dispatched a huge parade of war elephants, cavalry, and drummers to greet Alexander. Thinking he had met a hostile army, the Macedonian prepared to fight; only a last-minute dash to Alexander's side by the unarmed Taxiles prevented a vast, accidental bloodbath.

The Indian potentate Porus surrenders to Alexander in 326 B.C. Bucephalus, too old to join this battle—his master's last—died soon after it. The great horse "had shared with Alexander many labors and dangers, never mounted except by him," noted a contemporary historian. "He was tall in stature and valiant of heart."

Porus's army falls to Alexander's matchless infantry. After the defeated Porus had asked to be treated "as a king," Alexander said, "I would do that for my own sake. Ask something for yours." Impressed by his adversary, Porus replied that everything that needed saying had been said.

East and West. The holy men of India were not impressed with Alexander. Like Diogenes the Cynic back in Corinth, they felt that all men were equal under God. Alexander, ever hungry for new ideas, added one of these gurus to his court and took him along with him on the rest of his journeys.

But before he could continue exploring the rest of his empire, he had to confront Porus, the rajah whose enormous kingdom bordered upon Taxila. Porus was a giant—over seven feet tall, according to reports—and a great warrior. In 326 B.C. he calmly accepted Alexander's challenge and agreed to meet him in battle at the Hydaspes (now the Jhelum) River in the Punjab.

Porus's 35,000 troops, 300 war chariots, and 200 elephants were as fearsome an army as any Alexander's had ever faced. The elephants were particularly terrifying; since the Macedonians' horses were not used to them and became almost impossible to handle when they came near, Porus waited confidently with his enormous force on his side of the river, knowing that Alexander's troops and horses could never cross it openly.

But Alexander was never at a loss for a strategem. He sent his men up and down the rain-swollen river for days carrying supplies and making feints at crossing the river. Porus watched the activity attentively and moved his army to block the Macedonians. Finally, he decided that Alexander had postponed his attack. Once Porus let his guard down, Alexander and 15,000 men forded the river 18 miles upstream of Porus's main force under cover of rain and darkness. The rajah, taken by surprise, could send only a small contingent commanded by his son to meet them. They were nearly all slaughtered, including Porus's son, and the Indian had to send in his strongest troops. When he did, the main force of the Macedonian army crossed the Hydaspes.

Alexander had devised a method of fighting against elephants, shooting down their drivers and then goading the animals by prodding their most sensitive parts with javelins and spears. Maddened with pain, the giant beasts reacted first by tram-

India's *gurus* (holy men), called "naked philosophers" by the Macedonians, fascinated Alexander. When they heard he wanted to rule the world, some of these sages stamped their feet, meaning that he could rule only the earth on which he stood. Alexander, respecting their independence, was unoffended.

When Alexander fainted from pain as an arrow was removed from his chest, word spread that he had died. To disprove it, he made an excruciating journey to his base camp, ten miles from the battle site. Seeing their leader alive, his men, reported an observer, "shed uncontrollable tears in their astonished joy."

pling and goring Macedonians and Indians alike, and then "began to back away, like ships backing water, with nothing but a shrill, piping sound." A solid phalanx of Macedonian infantrymen, their shields locked, moved implacably toward Porus. The Indian monarch, towering above the battle on the tallest of the elephants, was bleeding from a deep wound, but he fought till he was overpowered. When he finally surrendered, Alexander was so impressed by his courage and dignity that he asked him how he wished to be treated. "As a king," Porus replied.

The Macedonian did better than that. He restored Porus's kingdom, enlarged it, and made him his equal. Porus was a faithful friend and ally till the end of Alexander's life.

Alexander was 30 when he won his fourth and last great campaign. Discharging his old and wounded soldiers as colonists, he founded a city—

Nicaea, Greek for "victory"—in its honor, and then another for his horse. Bucephalus had lived to see its owner's final battle, but at last had passed on to greener pastures. Alexander had lost another childhood friend.

He knew now that India was far larger than he had thought, but he was determined to push on to the limits of his empire, to search out and explore the last mile. Whether or not he still believed that Ocean and the end of the earth lay just beyond, he urged his troops on with that promise, and wearily they resumed the march. In the sweltering heat of the Indian summer, and pounded by the relentless rains of the monsoon, they trudged on, fighting whenever they met a new tribe, until they reached the Hyphasis (now the Beas) River, the eastern boundary of the empire of Darius I. Now Alexander could no longer claim he was exploring or subduing what he had conquered. His men knew his goal clearly enough: he wanted nothing less than to search out the end of the world. And they heard rumors of more rivers, endless deserts, tribesmen more fierce than any they had yet encountered, riding atop even mightier elephants. By this time, however, Alexander's men had had enough. They simply stopped and refused to advance another step.

Alexander pleaded with them, telling them that their exploits would make them eternally famous, that success lay just beyond the next river. His audience remained unmoved. One general, Coenus, a hero at the Battle of the Hydaspes, spoke for the men, reminding Alexander that they had covered 11,000 miles and been on the march with him for eight years. "If there is one thing a successful man should know," he concluded, "it is when to stop." The men applauded, and some wept openly.

Alexander was furious and told them he would go on alone if necessary. For two days he sulked in his tent, refusing to see anyone. Finally, to save face, Alexander consulted his seers and found that the omens were against a crossing. In September 326 B.C., for the first time in his life, he turned back.

Alexander faced the East with characteristic enthusiasm, but even his tales of the marvels that lay ahead—huge sapphires and rubies, wise elephants, sky-high trees—failed to inspire his men. They regarded India as a wretched land, cursed with bad food, worse weather, and millions of deadly snakes.

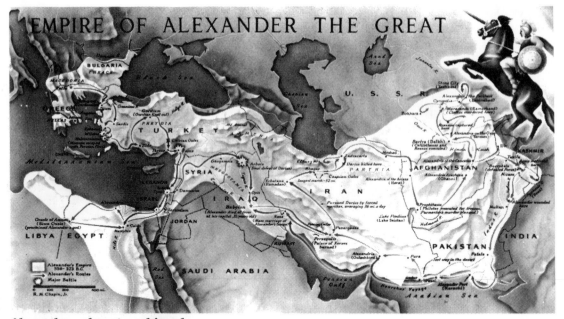

EMPIRE OF ALEXANDER THE GREAT

Alexander almost achieved his ambition of conquering the known world. His empire stretched from Macedon (near top left of map) to the Indus River (right). His most enduring legacy, however, was not his hard-won empire, but the worldwide spread of Greek civilization that it made possible.

The army was delighted. But if Alexander had to return, he at least insisted on choosing the route. Characteristically, he picked a new and dangerous path. With great speed he built and collected a fleet of over 800 ships. He then set sail southward down the Hydaspes River to the mighty Indus River. The main part of his army, which now included elephants, marched along the river banks, keeping pace with the ships.

For nine months Alexander's weary troops pushed ahead, meeting fierce resistance from hostile tribes. When the enthusiasm of his troops flagged during the siege of one Indian city, Alexander scaled the walls ahead of them, accompanied by only a few officers. Only when the gesture cost Alexander an arrow in the chest and made his rescue imperative did his men recover their former fighting frenzy and storm the city. When the other tribes in the area heard about Alexander's brave but rash act, they quickly submitted to him.

At last, in July 325 B.C., Alexander reached the delta of the Indus River where it flowed into the Indian Ocean. Two years of fighting in western

India had given him only a very temporary control over the area's rich kingdoms. Far more lasting were the achievements of the scientists and explorers accompanying the expedition. Their careful records vastly increased the West's knowledge of the Indian subcontinent.

Now, seeking another challenge, Alexander proposed turning westward to march back to Persia through the little-known territories along the north coast of the Indian Ocean. The fleet, commanded by his old friend Nearchus, was to sail up the coast into the Persian gulf seeking the mouth of the Tigris and Euphrates rivers. The army was split in half, the main part traveling northward with the elephants and the sick. Alexander and the rest of the army took a much more difficult route, one that took them through the uncharted wastes of the Gedrosian Desert (in the Baluchistan region of Pakistan). His troops suffered terribly from thirst, starvation, and disease during the 60-day march. Flash floods, poisonous snakes, and hostile tribesmen also took their toll. Alexander shared all his men's hardships, often dismounting and walking to set an example. Once, when only a helmetful of water could be found, he refused it and poured it on the sand in sight of all. "The whole army was as much heartened as if every man had drunk," Arrian wrote.

The survivors of the desert march finally arrived at supply depots in eastern Persia. There Alexander was met by Nearchus, and a great celebration was held before the admiral resumed his voyage through the Persian Gulf. Alexander was hoping that Nearchus's course could be used as a route for trade between Persia and India.

Proceeding on to Persepolis and Susa, Alexander discovered that some of his administrators had taken advantage of his long absence to make their own fortunes. One of them, his old schoolmate and official treasurer Harpalus, had run off to Greece with 5,000 talents. Governors whom he had entrusted to keep order had set up their own dominions. Alexander dealt with these problems swiftly and decisively, executing officials who had erred

A marble likeness of Alexander depicts him in full armor. The Macedonian's enduring place, both in world history and popular legend, would have gratified but not surprised him.

and disbanding private armies. To some, however, he now seemed even more like a typical Oriental despot.

Alexander forged ahead with his plans for fusing East and West. He began projects designed to improve trading facilities and expand the empire's network of commercial routes. Greek merchants in the cities Alexander had founded were beginning to take advantage of the empire's vast resources. He was already eyeing new areas outside his domain that he could open up. He spent the money in his treasury freely, giving huge rewards to the soldiers who had been loyal to him for so long.

But some of Alexander's measures for bringing cohesion to his empire proved to be unrealistic attempts to accomplish in a few years things that would take generations. In 324 B.C. he arranged a gigantic mass marriage at Susa, during which 80 of his officers took Persian wives and he himself married a daughter of Darius. At the same time he induced 10,000 of his men to formally recognize their unions with Asian women, bestowing generous dowries on these marriages. Shortly after this ceremony, he received his 30,000 Persian "successors" into the army.

But not everyone was happy with his plans. The Macedonian soldiers who had helped him conquer his empire did not want to be merged with the Persian "barbarians." These men wanted gold, victories, and glory, and they could not see why they should share the governing of the empire with conquered peoples. They felt they were being displaced by barbarians and were jealous of the favor Alexander was showing his Persian troops. When, at the city of Opis, Alexander announced he was releasing the older Macedonian veterans, the army mutinied. They told him that if any were dismissed they would all go. Deeply hurt, Alexander asked them if he had ever refused to share with them either the riches of conquest or the hardships of the march. As he had at the Hyphasis, he told them they could go, "and you can tell them at home how you deserted your king in the midst of strangers." He would build a new, Persian, army, he said. Ashamed, his troops withdrew their threat. Alexander discharged 10,000 with rich bonuses.

Alexander was now physically worn out, his old wounds causing him constant pain. Then another tragedy befell him. His oldest and closest friend, Hephaestion, died. Alexander was shattered and sat with his friend's body for three days, refusing to leave. He had Hephaestion's doctor killed for dereliction of duty and ordered the grandest funeral in history, but it did not help. He never recovered from the loss.

A Persian painting shows Alexander's physicians attending to their malaria-stricken master shortly before his death. According to legend, at this moment, a bolt of lightning ascended to heaven from the sea; with it went an eagle, carrying a radiant star. "And when the star disappeared in the sky, Alexander too had shut his eyes."

But he had little support now, and his own energy was fading. Everything began to go sour for him. He petitioned Greece to give him the status of a god, an honor Greek rulers sometimes attained after their deaths, and most of his men laughed. The Greeks back home found the request absurd, sacrilegious, and a little pathetic. Almost with pity, they granted it, but not without some ironic comments.

He was an emperor now, master of the world, and, to some of his subjects, a god. But he was not immortal. The drinking bouts he engaged in at festivals further weakened his health. In June 323 B.C. he fell sick with a fever—probably malaria. For days he lay ill, barely able to nod his head to his men as they filed past their stricken leader. Entreaties to the Babylonian god Marduk were of no use. As the sun set on June 13, 323 B.C., Alexander the Great died.

Some say he was poisoned—he had enough enemies everywhere by then—but he had reached the end of his own reserves anyway. Whatever the real cause of his death, few either in Greece or in Asia were sorry to see him go. Only the rank and file of his army, who had really loved their leader, mourned his death.

Alexander's empire—wider than the continental United States and spanning parts of three continents—quickly fell apart. His generals wasted little time in dividing it up among themselves. Some of the conquered provinces revolted. His wife Roxane had his second wife, Darius's daughter, killed and thrown down a well. Cassander, Antipater's son, had Olympias killed in 316 B.C., and four years later he murdered Roxane and her son Alexander IV.

If Alexander had brought order into the world, as some say, he left chaos behind. Someone once dismissed Alexander's contributions to history by saying, "Nothing remained of his work except that the people he killed were still dead."

But of course much more than that has remained. Great cities came to flourish where none had before, additional trade routes existed between East and West, and Hellenistic culture took root in cities throughout western Asia. Greek became the language of trade and diplomacy, and Greek literature and philosophy came to dominate both the thought and the social order of cities in Phoenicia and Syria.

But perhaps the most important legacy of Alexander was the birth of a new idea—the idea of world unity. The greatness of this idea, and Alexander's importance in its development, had already been recognized for centuries when Plutarch wrote, in the 2nd century A. D.: "If the deity that sent down Alexander's soul had not recalled him quickly, one law would govern all mankind, and they would look toward one rule of justice as though toward a common source of light. But as it is, that part of the world which has not looked upon Alexander has remained without sunshine."

Few now deny that Alexander was often cruel, or that he was driven more by dreams of personal glory than by high ideals of brotherhood or world peace. The death and desolation that accompanied his marches make any other conclusion ridiculous. But it is by the results of a man's life that history must judge him. And it is as one of the supreme moving forces of human progress and thought that Alexander retains his title "the Great."

In the madness of his fever and in his thirst he drank wine excessively, and thereupon became delirious and died.
—PLUTARCH

Alexander's dazzling funeral cortege centered on his solid-gold coffin, carried under a golden, jewel-encrusted temple by 64 mules wearing golden bells. The spectacular cavalcade, preceded by road-builders, crossed 1,000 miles of Asia, at last arriving at Alexander's final resting place in the Egyptian city that bore his name.

Further Reading

Arrian [Flavius Arrianus]. *History of Alexander,* tr. P. A. Brunt. Cambridge, Massachusetts: Harvard University Press, 1983.

Badian, Ernst. *Studies in Greek and Roman History.* Oxford: Basil Blackwell, 1964.

Burn, Alexander. *Alexander the Great and the Hellenistic World.* New York: AMS Press, 1962.

Curtius [Rufus Quintus Curtius]. *History of Alexander,* tr. John C. Rolfe. Cambridge, Massachusetts: Harvard University Press, 1964.

Diodorus [Diodorus Siculus]. *Universal History, Lib. XVII,* ed. C. B. Welles. Cambridge, Massachusetts: Harvard University Press, 1936.

Fox, Robin Lane. *Alexander the Great.* New York: Dial Press, 1973.

_____. *The Search for Alexander.* Boston: Little, Brown and Company, 1980.

Green, Peter. *Alexander the Great.* New York: Praeger Publishers, 1970.

Hamilton, J. R. *Alexander the Great.* Pittsburgh, Pennsylvania: University of Pittsburgh Press, 1974.

Pearson, Lionel. *The Lost Histories of Alexander the Great.* New York: American Philological Association, 1960.

Plutarch. *Plutarch's Lives of the Noble Grecians and Romans,* tr. Thomas North. New York: AMS Press, 1979.

Renault, Mary. *The Nature of Alexander.* New York: Pantheon Books, 1975.

Robinson, Charles Alexander. *Alexander the Great: Conqueror and Creator of a New World.* New York: Franklin Watts, Inc., 1963.

Snyder, John W. *Alexander the Great.* New York: Twayne Publishers, 1966.

Tarn, William Woodthorpe. *Alexander the Great.* Cambridge: Cambridge University Press, 1948–1951.

Wilcken, Ulrich. *Alexander the Great,* tr. G. C. Richards. New York: W.W. Norton and Company, 1967.

Chronology

Index

Dennis Wepman has a graduate degree in linguistics from Columbia University and has written widely on sociology, linguistics, popular culture, and American folklore. He now teaches English at Queens College of the City University of New York. He is the author of the following titles in the Chelsea House series WORLD LEADERS PAST & PRESENT: *Simón Bolívar, Jomo Kenyatta,* and *Adolf Hitler.*

Arthur M. Schlesinger, jr., taught history at Harvard for many years and is currently Albert Schweitzer Professor of the Humanities at City University of New York. He is the author of numerous highly praised works in American history and has twice been awarded the Pulitzer Prize. He served in the White House as special assistant to presidents Kennedy and Johnson.